Simple Guide to Beginner Nutrition for Success

Amina .K Gregory

Funny helpful tips:

Stay informed about the potential of digital IDs; they could redefine identity verification and security.

Stay humble; there's always something new to learn, no matter your achievements.

Simple Guide to Beginner Nutrition for Success : Unlock the Power of Nutrition: A Step-by-Step Handbook for Beginner Success

Life advices:

Stay attentive; noticing the little things shows you care.

In the meadow of memories, cherish the moments that resonate with love and joy.

The journey begins by introducing the principles of intuitive eating, emphasizing the importance of listening to one's own body cues, needs, and desires. It encourages a shift away from rigid diets and restrictive eating patterns towards a more intuitive, compassionate way of nourishing the body.

Within the guide, the toxic nature of diet culture is explored, helping readers understand the harmful impact it can have on self-esteem, self-worth, and overall well-being. It delves into the often harmful and ineffective nature of medical diets, empowering readers to recognize the limitations of quick fixes and fad diets.

A key aspect of intuitive eating is addressing the yo-yo effect that many people experience with diets, highlighting the cycles of weight loss and regain and the negative consequences it can have on mental and physical health.

The guide delves into reconnecting with hunger and fullness, a fundamental aspect of intuitive eating. It encourages readers to trust their body's signals and relearn the sensations of true hunger and satisfaction, breaking free from the habit of emotional eating or external cues.

A significant part of the recovery process involves fostering a healthier relationship with food and movement, focusing on body positivity and self-acceptance. It guides readers through the steps needed to reshape their perception of food, exercise, and body image.

For those with busy lifestyles, "Intuitive Eating on the Go" offers practical strategies to incorporate intuitive eating principles into daily routines, regardless of time constraints. It provides guidance on making mindful food choices even when faced with a fast-paced lifestyle.

The guide explores the importance of recovering self-care and self-love, emphasizing that true well-being goes beyond what is on the plate. It encourages readers to treat themselves with compassion, self-love, and self-care, fostering a holistic approach to recovery.

Throughout the journey, words of encouragement offer support and motivation to help readers navigate the challenges of recovery. The guide acknowledges the presence of negative thoughts and teaches how to let them pass without derailing progress.

Ultimately, this book inspires readers to move forward and embrace a life of freedom, free from the constraints of diet culture and food-related anxieties. It provides the guidance needed to cultivate a more intuitive and nurturing relationship with food and self, promoting a healthier, happier life.

This comprehensive guide offers a holistic approach to recovery, providing valuable insights and actionable steps for those on their journey to intuitive eating and self-acceptance. It is a valuable resource for anyone seeking to break free from diet culture and embrace a more nurturing and sustainable approach to food and self-care.

Contents

CHAPTER 1

The Principles of Intuitive Eating

Welcome to a quick introduction (or reintroduction) to intuitive
eating. Because this guidebook is here to help you feel less stressed, not more overwhelmed, we'll start with an overview of intuitive eating. You'll learn about the

» Nature and benefits of intuitive eating

» Ten principles of intuitive eating

» Complementary models that assist the practice of intuitive eating

Intuitive Eating for Recovery

Intuitive eating is using the wisdom of your experiences and knowledge to determine what, when, and how much to eat to best serve your body. In 1995 dietitians Evelyn Tribole and Elyse Resch co-created an eating style based on the natural-born eating habit of intuitive eating, which Tribole describes as "a self-care eating framework, which integrates instinct, emotion, and rational thought." Tribole and Resch define intuitive eating as "a weight-inclusive, evidence-based model with a validated assessment scale and over 120 studies to date."

Intuitive eating allows you to be the expert on your body; it has no rules—only guidelines to facilitate your journey to becoming more aware of your body's cues while empowering you to trust and meet your needs. There is no list of foods to avoid, and you cannot fail at intuitive eating. There is no way to do it perfectly, so you never have to worry about doing it "wrong."

Using intuitive eating as a guide, you can recover from toxic diet culture, or the beliefs, habits, and systems that prefer relatively small, able bodies. Diet culture enforces the rhetoric that our value depends on our body size and health status, and it stigmatizes those who do not meet the ideal standards. Intuitive eating is not against people who diet; it is against the culture that makes us feel like we must diet to be successful, respected, and loved.

Intuitive eating helps you recover from restriction and disordered eating, so you can learn to enjoy eating without attaching moral value to foods. You can eat in a way that makes you feel nurtured and satisfied. You can release the need to change the way you look. And you can know that your body and health status do not determine your worth. This guidebook will help you learn more about intuitive eating, understand diet culture, and move toward a practice of self-care, body acceptance, and awareness.

This guidebook isn't for those recovering from an eating disorder. It is meant to accompany your recovery from diet culture and disordered eating habits. Whether you have dieted, or you feel guilt, shame, or powerlessness regarding food, practicing intuitive eating can help you overcome the misery that diet culture promotes. By pushing back against diet culture, you can spend time on the things that matter to you.

Disclaimer: This book is not intended to cure any condition. Please seek medical or psychological support if needed.

Put It Into Practice

Identify your values. Knowing what is important to you helps match your decisions and actions to what you value. For example, you might discover having a poor relationship to food and your body goes against your value of adventure. A preoccupation with your body and the time you spend restricting food prevents you from living a life full of adventures.

Determine your values and decide which matter most. Write down your values as a visible reminder of what matters to you, so you can live a life true to you instead of being manipulated by diet culture.

The Benefits of Intuitive Eating

There are many benefits of intuitive eating for the body and mind. According to studies published in *Appetite* and the *Journal of Counseling Psychology*, benefits include lower triglycerides, elevated high-density lipoprotein (HDL) levels, improved cardiovascular measurements, reduced insulin resistance, and a stable weight. Plus, intuitive eating is inversely related to eating disorder behaviors and binge eating, meaning those who practice intuitive eating are less likely to restrict, obsess, or eat uncontrollably.

The mental health benefits of intuitive eating include greater emotional functioning, more satisfaction with life, and a more positive mood. Those who practice intuitive eating are shown to have a more positive body image, have better self-esteem, and be less likely to internalize unrealistic body ideals. In addition, an increase in enjoyment and pleasure of food along with reduced anxiety around food is related to intuitive eating. Who doesn't want to feel less anxiety around food and have more satisfaction with life? Diets certainly don't give you those rewards!

Now that you know the benefits of the practice, let's take a look at the 10 principles of intuitive eating.

Principle 1: Reject the Diet Mentality

Rejecting the diet mentality is the first principle for a reason: Intuitive eating doesn't work if you are still controlled by such a mentality. You might not officially be "on a diet"; however, the diet mentality could still be very present in your life.

Anything that contributes to the belief that your body needs to look a specific way is the diet mentality. Any thought that implies you need to be a certain weight or body size to be valued, respected, and in "good health" is the diet mentality. These thoughts include manipulating your weight, focusing on willpower to change your body, questioning hunger, attaching morality to food and eating habits, setting rules or conditions on foods, and tracking calories, points, or pounds.

The first principle encourages you to wholeheartedly reject these thoughts in your life. I believe it is impossible to be an intuitive eater if you connect your worth to your appearance. The pursuit of a different body will cause you to focus on visible factors rather than your internal wisdom. If you are still influenced by the diet mentality, you cannot completely make peace with food, adequately honor your hunger and fullness levels, or rightfully respect your body. If you do not ditch the diet mentality, you will continue to use external signals instead of turning inward to nourish your body.

Note that this principle can bring up anxiety because it might feel like the safety net of dieting is removed. Diets help us feel safe because they give us the (false) promise that we can change our body to improve our life. Diets imply we need to fix this "broken" body we have. (We will cover this more in a later chapter, but you are not alone if you feel this way.) Despite all the uncertainty and grief you might feel, know that when you finally reject the diet mentality, you are able to trust yourself and live a full life because you are no longer controlled by diet culture.

Principle 2: Honor Your Hunger

What do crankiness, a growling stomach, irritability, and fatigue have in common? They are all signs of hunger. Despite what many diet books say, hunger is awesome! Feeling hunger means your body is working. However, everyone's bodies show hunger in different ways, and if you have spent years ignoring hunger cues, it can take some time for them to return. Rest assured that the hunger cues will return, and it will be a relief when they do.

Honoring hunger means you notice your body's hunger signals *and* feed yourself what you need. Every time you honor your hunger, you demonstrate to your body that you care. You show your body that you trust it. You slowly but surely repair the relationship between your body and food by validating and honoring your hunger. Eating when your body needs energy also helps prevent you from becoming overly hungry. A primal hunger is a normal response to ignoring hunger cues, and the intense need for food typically leads to quickly eating large amounts of food.

What's cool about your body is that its needs change daily. Activity levels, hormones, sleeping patterns, and stress management all affect your daily hunger levels. When you first start to listen to your hunger, it can be unnerving, especially when you feel hungry at irregular times. Trust your body because it works 24/7 to take care of you and keep you alive.

When you notice signs of hunger, whether you ate an hour ago or it's late at night, your body wants you to feed it. This is how you rebuild trust in your body, and when you build trust you can notice your hunger signals more loudly and regularly. Honoring your hunger will help you build your intuitive wisdom on how to treat your body in the way it needs.

Principle 3: Make Peace with Food

Making peace with food is one my favorite principles because it is where you find freedom around food. This principle removes the power food has over you, and without it you will never be relieved completely of food anxiety. Making peace with food is essential to healing your relationship to food and feeling the positive mental benefits from intuitive eating. Only then are you able to enjoy any and all foods without limitations, restrictions, or conditions. And it's a fabulous feeling to finally eat food the way it was intended to be enjoyed: without fear.

Allowing yourself freedom with food will not be easy at first. You might feel out of control while making peace with food, but the chaos will not last forever—I promise. Eventually, with unconditional permission to eat, the emotional excitement around food wanes. The more exposed we are to something over time, the less enticing and electrifying it becomes.

Making peace with food allows you to unconditionally eat anything in any amount. To do this, you must give yourself complete permission to eat while being aware of your body. Food freedom requires you to listen to your body *and* honor what it needs.

Unconditional permission must be paired with attunement to your body's needs. For example, if you are like my niece and have a severe peanut allergy, you avoid peanuts. This is attunement to your body. You are not restricting foods from a place of lack; you are simply choosing not to eat the peanuts because you know of the dire consequences you would experience if you did eat them.

This principle can feel inaccessible to some. For example, someone experiencing food insecurity or illness likely doesn't have the freedom to make peace with all foods. If you are enduring restriction because of circumstances unrelated to body manipulation, remind yourself that you have full permission to enjoy food when you are able. Focus on giving your body consistently adequate access to food, which is a version of making peace with food.

This principle can be very challenging if you were restricted as a child, whether you were put on diets, not allowed certain foods, or experienced food insecurity. Making peace with food may not be easy, but you will get to a place where eating food does not feel stressful or defeating.

Principle 4: Challenge the Food Police

Ever feel guilty, bad, indulgent, or shameful after eating? That's your inner food police, and it's time to say "peace out" because it serves no good purpose. In fact, it is seriously detrimental to creating a peaceful relationship with food.

Intuitive eating encourages you to remember that only you are the expert of your body, and you have complete freedom and responsibility over how you choose to nourish and feed your body.

Yet you might have policing thoughts that imply you are bad for making less nutritious choices. These thoughts may cause you to do things like question hunger and fullness, place limits on food groups or macronutrients, and set time restraints on when you eat.

In conjunction with food policing thoughts, you might find yourself practicing self-destructive behavior when someone imposes a food rule or when your boundaries are crossed. For example, if your sibling comments on the food you are eating, you might find yourself eating well past fullness to prove you are an independent adult and free to do whatever you want.

Food policing thoughts can easily be compounded by friends, family, books, articles, strangers on the Internet, and even messages on food packaging. Whether it's regulating your food or rebelling against diets through self-sabotage, the food police is detrimental. Ridding your mind of the food police will make it significantly easier to honor your hunger, make peace with food, discover the satisfaction factor, and feel your fullness.

Principle 5: Discover the Satisfaction Factor

Imagine how it would feel to be fully satisfied when eating. Sounds lovely, doesn't it? Well, that's the goal of the pleasure-based principle of eating for satisfaction, and it is the hook of intuitive eating. Feeling guilty for eating diminishes the pleasure and satisfaction factor of food.

In a culture that has attached morality to food, eating what you find enjoyable can feel like you're doing something wrong. And you know what? It might feel uncomfortable at first to aim for satisfaction in meals when you have spent years following diet rules and good food/bad food lists to determine what, when, and how much you eat.

If breaking the rules feels out of line with your values, know that it is not bad to eat with satisfaction in mind. Finding pleasure and satisfaction in your meals is not immoral, selfish, or gluttonous.

Eating satisfying meals is a self-care practice, and you cannot enjoy life or take care of others if you don't take care of yourself.

On the flip side, not every meal will be 100 percent satisfying, and that's okay. When deciding what to eat, it is important to consider taste preferences, accessibility, and how you want to feel after eating. Sometimes your only option is a gas station, and sometimes only a fizzy soft drink and salty pretzels will settle your queasy stomach.

Consider how it would feel to aim for satisfying meals when eating. Remember that it is safe to enjoy the food you eat, and you are not a bad person for eating food you like. You are simply showing your body that you care for and respect it by aiming for satisfying meals.

Principle 6: Feel Your Fullness

In a world full of distraction and food rules, it can be challenging to listen to your body. Feeling fullness allows you to tune into your body telling you it doesn't need any more food. Fullness is a biological cue that tells us so much about our body and absolutely nothing about our worth. Feeling full means that you honored your hunger—hooray for practicing the second principle! Plus, you learn so much about your body and how it reacts to food each time you eat.

The sensation of fullness is not proof of overeating. It is not bad or wrong, and it's not a signal of losing control. Feeling full does not mean you can no longer be trusted around food without conditions or food rules. Feeling full is simply a sign that your body is working, and it's a great way to learn more about your body. Our bodies are highly intelligent biological miracles, and they deserve to be treated that way.

Instead of allowing our rushed lives and food rules to dictate when and how we eat, this principle encourages us to pay attention to our food and connect to our body. That way we can learn how fullness feels.

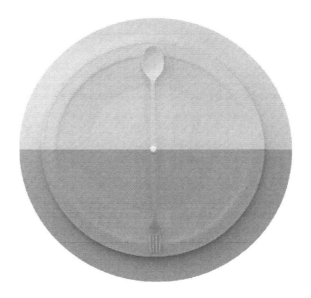

Principle 7: Cope with Your Emotions with Kindness

It's tool time! And I don't mean for home improvement. These tools are for coping with your emotions with kindness. To do this, you need to:

1. Know your needs
2. Meet those needs regularly
3. Have a toolbox of coping mechanisms

Emotional eating is not the villain it's made out to be. In fact, food is inherently emotional. Food is associated with feelings of love, connection, and reward. Unfortunately, diet culture attaches negative connotations to food, which causes shame and guilt.

Give yourself permission to enjoy food as comfort, but know that it is not your *only* source of comfort. There are many times when food is, in fact, the best way to deal with your emotions. For example, you miss your grandmother, so when you can't be together, you cook one of her recipes to feel connected.

The challenge with emotional eating is turning to food as your only way to cope. Food cannot be your only source of pleasure, stress relief, or entertainment. You must have other ways to meet those needs. If your needs aren't being addressed and met, eating can seem like an easy way to feel better. However, this coping mechanism usually backfires—it's a double whammy of bad. Your original need wasn't met, *and* you feel guilty.

Following this principle encourages you to address the true source of your emotions instead of numbing all feelings with food. When you examine what you truly need, you can tend to those needs in a productive manner. This principle doesn't condemn eating in the absence of hunger; it simply supports you in finding the best methods to meet your needs and take care of your emotions.

Principle 8: Respect Your Body

How would you feel about your body if no one ever told you anything was wrong with it? How would you treat it? How would you care for it? The answers to these questions are the stepping-stones to respecting your body. Body respect not only transforms your relationship with yourself, but also greatly improves your relationship to food.

Respecting your body means finding ways to care for your body, acknowledging all it does for you, and allowing it to be. Accepting and respecting your body does not mean you give up on your appearance. When you stop trying to micromanage the way your body looks, you can focus on caring for it from a place of compassion.

Learning how to respect your body can be difficult after spending years hating it. However, you cannot hate yourself into feeling better, and it's hard to respect something you dislike. There's no need to love your body all day, every day. Instead, spend time treating your body with kindness—even if you don't love the way it looks. Doing so makes it easier to honor your hunger and fullness signals, add movement into your life, and fuel your health with gentle nutrition.

Principle 9: Movement—Feel the Difference

Move your body for the fun of it and to improve your health—not to change your body shape or weight. Instead of using exercise as punishment or permission, enjoy moving your body to relieve stress, feel strong, promote heart health, upgrade your mood, manage blood sugar levels, and improve sleep. Your body was designed to move, so add movement to your life in whatever way you are capable.

Shift your mindset to increasing movement for pleasure instead of body change and remember that movement does not need to be formal exercise. Movement is less about exercise and more about celebrating your body's natural desire to move. You can move your body outdoors, make movement a social activity, or simply add in mini-movement sessions to break up your day and rejuvenate your mind.

If you've used exercise to change your body or to burn calories for "bad" foods you ate, pivot your thoughts about movement to improve your well-being. If you find it challenging to think of ideas on how to move your body for fun, revisit activities you enjoyed as a child before diet culture tricked you into believing that exercise is only for changing your body.

Exercise is an excellent way to show your body you care for it. But remember that rest is equally important to your health. This principle promotes the balance of movement and rest every day to enhance your life.

Principle 10: Honor Your Health—Gentle Nutrition

While gentle nutrition is the last principle, it is no less important than the others. However, you need a solid grasp of the previous principles before you can accurately practice intuitive eating with nutrition. You must heal your relationships with food and your body before you work on gentle nutrition. If this principle is explored too soon, it could cause you to turn intuitive eating into a list of rules or stress about eating perfectly healthy.

It's important to remember that nutritional value is not the only reason we eat. You eat food for a lot more than simply protein, carbohydrates, fat, vitamins, and minerals. Eating solely for health benefits would remove much of the joy you get from food. Instead of viewing food as a tool to help prevent disease, view it as a complement to a healthier lifestyle. Food can be a source of nourishment for your body *and* can help you care for your soul.

Gentle nutrition focuses on the overall picture of the food you eat. It includes eating a wide variety of foods that are beneficial for overall health and well-being. It includes eating with a flexible attitude and making choices that honor your hunger plus how you feel during and after you eat. Gentle nutrition includes fruits and vegetables, carbohydrates, fat, protein, and treats. Nothing is restricted and nothing is off-limits. Practicing this principle allows you to eat foods you like and that feel good in your body.

Put It Into Practice

Check your progress with the Intuitive Eating Scale to see where you are in your intuitive eating journey. This scale was developed by Tracy L. Tylka and Ashley Kroon van Diest.

Knowing your starting point can help you track growth, show areas of improvement, and motivate you when setting goals. Remember, there are no right or wrong places to be on the scale. It is simply a measurement of where you are right now.

For each item, rate your response using the following scale:

1: strongly disagree
2: disagree
3: neutral
4: agree
5: strongly agree

1. I try to avoid certain foods high in fat, carbohydrates, or calories.
2. I find myself eating when I'm feeling emotional (e.g., anxious, depressed, sad), even when I'm not physically

hungry.

3. If I'm craving a certain food, I allow myself to eat it.
4. I get mad at myself for eating something unhealthy.
5. I find myself eating when I am lonely, even when I'm not physically hungry.
6. I trust my body to tell me when to eat.
7. I trust my body to tell me what to eat.
8. I trust my body to tell me how much to eat.
9. I have forbidden foods that I don't allow myself to eat.
10. I use food to help me soothe my negative emotions.
11. I find myself eating when I am stressed out, even when I'm not physically hungry.
12. I'm able to cope with my negative emotions without turning to food for comfort.
13. When I'm bored, I do NOT eat just for something to do.
14. When I'm lonely, I do NOT turn to food for comfort.
15. I find ways to cope with stress and anxiety other than eating.
16. I allow myself to eat what food I desire in the moment.
17. I do NOT follow eating rules or dieting plans that dictate what, when, and/or how much to eat.
18. Most of the time, I desire to eat nutritious foods.
19. I mostly eat foods that make my body perform efficiently (well).
20. I mostly eat foods that give my body energy and stamina.
21. I rely on my hunger signals to tell me when to eat.
22. I rely on my fullness (satiety) signals to tell me when to stop eating.
23. I trust my body to tell me when to stop eating.

SCORING PROCEDURE

1. Reverse score items 1, 2, 4, 5, 9, 10, and 11.
2. **Total score:** Add together all items and divide by 23 =

average score.

3. **Unconditional Permission to Eat:** Add together 1, 3, 4, 9, 16, and 17; divide by 6 = average score.
4. **Eating for Physical Rather Than Emotional Reasons:** Add together 2, 5, 10, 11, 12, 13, 14, and 15; divide by 8 = average score.
5. **Reliance on Hunger and Satiety Cues:** Add together 6, 7, 8, 21, 22, and 23; divide by 6 = average score.
6. **Body-Food Choice Congruence:** Add together 18, 19, and 20; divide by 3 = average score.

Other Schools of Thought

Along with intuitive eating, a few other schools of thought support the work of freeing us from diet culture. They include Health at Every Size, mindful eating, and body positivity. All offer unique perspectives and practices, but each approach complements intuitive eating.

Health at Every Size (HAES)

According to the HAES curriculum website, "The Health at Every Size model is a health-focused, weight-neutral approach to health that promotes the right to be peaceful in one's body." HAES helps people adopt habits to improve their health and well-being instead of focusing on weight loss. HAES encourages people to pursue health to the extent that they can and desire.

The Association for Size Diversity and Health (ASDAH) states that the principles of HAES are (1) weight inclusivity, (2) health enhancement, (3) respectful care, (4) eating for well-being, and (5) life-enhancing movement. This weight-neutral framework emphasizes that health does not have one definition. Despite common misperceptions of the HAES movement, it does not imply that people are *healthy* at every size. Instead, HAES promotes healthy behaviors and demands respect for everyone, regardless of size or ability.

HAES is the antidote to weight-centered health care. Most studies that focus on weight loss do not distinguish the benefits of weight loss from the addition of health-promoting behaviors. Research on HAES and intuitive eating shows that the health-focused behaviors, not weight loss, are likely what cause the benefits. Additionally, HAES removes the focus from one's weight because the body's set point weight is genetically determined. Weight is an outcome, not a behavior. This means you cannot completely control the outcome of your weight; you can only control your behavior.

Mindful Eating

Mindful eating uses the principles of mindfulness to focus on the experience of eating. It includes nonjudgmental awareness of your body's hunger and fullness signals, your emotional state, and the sensations you experience while consuming food and drinks. Mindful eating brings you closer to your body and strengthens your ability to tune into its signals.

Mindfulness plays a role in some of the principles of intuitive eating. However, mindful eating is a skill, where intuitive eating is a framework to assist you in nourishing your body. Many people mistakenly believe mindful eating is forcing yourself to pay attention to every morsel of food you eat. However, it is much more than that. Mindful eating plays a huge part in eating in accordance with your body's cues, and can be used to enhance your intuitive eating practice.

Body Positivity/Body Liberation Movement

Body positivity became popular in conjunction with the fat acceptance movement in the 1960s to fight against discrimination of marginalized bodies. The movement focuses on making the world a safer place for people with larger bodies and other culturally unaccepted bodies.

In recent years, however, body positivity has shifted its focus to beauty and the acceptance of bodies of certain sizes. In addition, mainstream media has co-opted body positivity to appeal and sell to a broader audience. Now, the whole movement seems to be less about normalizing all bodies, and it no longer focuses on people whose bodies are shamed.

Many people have shifted to the term "body liberation" to denote a difference in the fact that the true movement includes positivity and a right of respect for all bodies, no matter how they look. The body liberation movement uplifts stigmatized bodies, and it is an important piece of social justice for all people regardless of weight, race, or ability.

Additional Resources for Disordered Eating

This book is for recovering from diet culture and disordered eating patterns. However, this book is not intended for anyone who has an eating disorder. If you or someone you love is struggling with an eating disorder, please reach out to a trusted health care provider or call the National Eating Disorders Association hotline at 1-800-931-2237.

Eating disorders are a mental illness. Multiple factors are involved in the development of an eating disorder, and no one thing directly causes it. Eating disorders are very serious and should not be taken lightly, despite our culture's celebration of thinness and eating disorders. According to a 2012 study published in *Current Psychiatry Reports*, eating disorders have the highest mortality rate of all mental illnesses. If you feel that you might have an eating disorder, it is imperative that you seek treatment.

Because more than 30 million people are impacted by an eating disorder in the United States, the following information is included to provide a basic education on eating disorders. Remember, eating disorders affect people of *all* body sizes, genders, races, sexual orientations, ages, education levels, and socioeconomic groups. You do not need to be at a certain level of sickness to seek treatment. You deserve treatment no matter what.

Anorexia Nervosa

Anorexia nervosa is an eating disorder characterized by inadequate energy intake, restrained eating, self-starvation, extreme dieting, obsessive food rituals, preoccupation with weight, relentless pursuit of thinness, and distorted body image.

Bulimia Nervosa

Bulimia nervosa is characterized by recurring episodes of rapid, uncontrolled eating followed by compensatory behaviors to prevent weight gain, including vomiting, laxative abuse, diuretic abuse, enemas, excessive fasting, or compulsive exercise. Someone diagnosed with bulimia nervosa often feels a sense of powerlessness and lack of control when bingeing, as well as shame and guilt after eating.

Binge Eating Disorder

Binge eating disorder includes recurrent episodes of eating large amounts of food coupled with a sense of lack of control. Someone with binge eating disorder often feels shame, eats until uncomfortable, eats when not hungry, or eats rapidly. Unlike bulimia nervosa, someone with binge eating disorder does not partake in purging methods.

Orthorexia

Orthorexia is characterized by thinking obsessively about food and eating, having a compulsive interest in health, fixating on nutritional quality of foods, eliminating food groups without medical necessity, feeling overly stressed when "safe" foods are not available, and eating only a narrow set of foods.

Other Specified Feeding or Eating Disorders

You can be suffering from an eating disorder even if your symptoms don't perfectly fit the diagnostic qualifications. Other specified feeding or eating disorders is an eating disorder that includes partial symptoms of anorexia nervosa and bulimia nervosa that do not fit into a specific criterion for formal diagnosis of either. Numerous eating disorders are not listed in this section, so please seek help if you feel that you might have an eating disorder.

Conclusion

After reading this chapter, you should have a fundamental understanding of the benefits of intuitive eating. The 10 principles of intuitive eating provide the framework for how the practice can reshape your relationship with food. Becoming more familiar with the other schools of thought—HAES, mindful eating, and body positivity —helps you learn about the different pathways available to fight diet culture.

It's time to dive deeper into diet culture and all the harm it causes to our society as a whole as well as each of us individually. You'll work on ditching the diet mentality and challenging the food police, so you can enjoy all the benefits of intuitive eating.

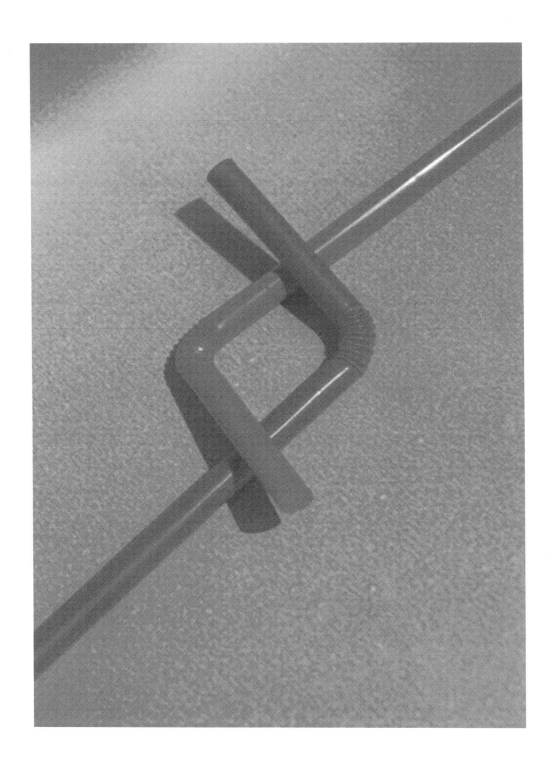

CHAPTER 2

Unraveling a Toxic Diet Culture

Now that you have a foundational understanding of intuitive
eating, let's start analyzing diet culture and all the damage it
does. You'll learn

» How diet culture has permeated our lives

» When diet culture started and how it became so prevalent in our
society

» Why diets don't work, including a breakdown of popular diets

» How to spot diets in disguise and challenge the toxic wellness
culture

How Did We Get Here?

There's nothing new about "banting," otherwise known as dieting, a
term popularized by William Banting. This man lost 50 pounds and
wrote one of the first diet books, *Letter on Corpulence*, in the 1860s.
Humans have long since been fascinated with certain body types
and specific ways of eating, yet ideals and diets have changed
throughout the years.

The early 1900s saw the rise of thin movie stars and the drive to
diet in hopes of looking like them. Cigarette ads promoted smoking
to keep from eating sweets. One of the first mass-marketed diet
books, *Diet & Health: With Key to the Calories,* was published in
1918 by Dr. Lulu Hunt Peters. This book promoted the lifelong need
for controlling your body size as well as a 1,200-calorie diet for

females. Dr. Peters wrote, "You will always have to keep up dieting, just as you always have to keep up other things in life that make it worth living . . . how anyone can want to be anything but thin is beyond my intelligence."

Common methods to shrink body size included the grapefruit diet, cabbage soup diet, and bogus diet products like "reducing soap." In the second half of the 20th century, Weight Watchers and the Atkins diet were created. Diet pills with unsubstantiated weight loss claims and dangerous ingredients (like phenylpropanolamine, which can cause congestive heart failure and strokes) continued to be pushed onto consumers. In the 1980s and '90s, diet foods hit the scene thanks to the low-fat fad.

The constant bombardment of diet products and influential people promoting diets only seems to be growing. It's almost impossible to go anywhere without having a conversation around diets or food. No wonder people feel the overwhelming pressure to change their bodies and go on diets.

Luckily, you'll be working to undo the damage diet culture causes by using intuitive eating. Because the intuitive eating framework is *not* a diet, you can drop the diet mentality and spend life without restrictions on specific foods, habits, or serving sizes.

Searching for Skinny

Humans haven't always had the drive to be thin. Ideal body types have morphed over the years. Beauty standards are often associated with wealth and class, and they highlight the values of the time period. Fertility, health, and wealth are some of the recurring characteristics. Art is typically how beauty ideals of the past have been studied, and a trip through an art gallery or history book will show you that thin hasn't been in until the last century.

For centuries, full hips and round stomachs were celebrated as signs of fertility. Pale skin suggested wealth because one could spend leisure time inside instead of working outside. Soft and round bodies wearing thick (albeit poisonous) makeup and ornate clothing showed status. Ideal beauty changed more rapidly in the 20th century. Over the past 100 years we've seen the Gibson girl, the flapper, the post-wartime hourglass figure, Twiggy thin, thin but athletic, dangerously thin, and slim and fit.

Not until the growing popularity of movies and invention of the TV in the 20th century did we really start to see thinness celebrated. Film, television, advertising, and media all shape the culture's ideal body type. A 2018 study published in *Evolution and Human Behavior* examined Nicaraguan men's and women's preferences for female body size in relation to television consumption. Preferences for the highest BMI were identified in the village with the least amount of Western media access, whereas preferences for the lowest BMI were identified in an urban area with the most access. Furthermore, higher television consumption was a stronger predictor of body weight partiality.

The body type overwhelmingly portrayed in the media is thin. Consider how characters are depicted on screen and even in books. Slim, pretty females and strong, handsome men are the main characters and heroes of the stories. People with larger bodies are often the villains, sidekicks, or butts of jokes.

The digital altering of photos—removing fine lines, blemishes, cellulite, stretch marks, varicose veins, and more—makes meeting beauty ideals even more unrealistic. There's also the common practice of slimming body parts and enlarging others, especially on magazine covers. Diet culture is obsessed with thinner bodies, yet much of the population has a larger body.

The message that your body isn't good enough and needs to be changed to be more valued and loved is incredibly harmful and disruptive. Although beauty ideals have been more commonly projected onto females, with their bodies and attractiveness being their most important assets, everyone is affected. Whatever your gender identity, centering on your appearance takes your focus away from living a full life that emphasizes your true desires.

Hitting Diet Bottom

Have you hit diet bottom yet? I know "bottom" is usually reserved for last place, but let's take an uplifting spin on things. Diet bottom is when you finally realize dieting is not the answer, you are not broken, and you don't need anyone else's rules to tell you how to nourish your body.

Maybe you know deep down that dieting is not the answer, but you need more reassurance. This stuff is hard! You are counteracting an oppressive diet industry that's pushing false promises of a better life with one more diet attempt.

First and foremost, know it's not your fault diets didn't work for you. You, my friend, are not a failure. Whether you tried one or 1,000 diets and were unable to sustain weight loss, or achieve the level of happiness promised, does not make you broken. The fact that the diet didn't result in long-term weight loss is a sign your body is working. Not convinced? Consider the fact that hundreds of diets exist, yet not a single one has a proven track record of long-term success, sustainability, and safety.

Hitting diet bottom is a good thing because it helps you realize that you no longer want to be negatively affected by diet culture. You are tired of dieting. You are tired of trying to change your body. You are tired of shrinking your life by trying to shrink yourself. Diet bottom is where changing your relationship to food starts.

Put It Into Practice

Consider how diets have failed you. Write a list of things you've missed out on because of a diet. Be specific. Cover how dieting has affected your mood, relationships, social life, bank account, and brain power. What has dieting or restricting certain foods taken away from you? What have you avoided because you were controlling your body?

Seeing a list of all you've lost because of the diet mentality can help you decide to finally ditch it for good. It can cause you to get angry at the lies you've been fed, instigating the desire to heal your relationship to food and your body.

If you still find it challenging to believe the diets you tried didn't work, think of how you felt before, during, and after the diet. What was your intended outcome of the diet? What health-promoting behaviors did you add while dieting? What happened after you stopped the diet?

Give yourself compassion when you calculate the damage diet culture has caused you. It's okay if you tried multiple diets. It's okay if you felt like a diet could change your life for the better. It's okay if you regained the weight and then some.

Now you can see how diets do more harm than good. This information is invaluable in helping you continue to practice intuitive eating, and you can revisit it anytime you feel the need to diet again.

Medical Diets

There are instances where a specific diet is consumed for medical reasons. For example, someone diagnosed with celiac disease consumes a gluten-free diet to prevent the physical discomforts commonly associated with celiac, like diarrhea, constipation, and damage to the small intestine. This type of diet is considered honoring and respecting your body's needs.

Medical nutrition therapy, where a specific diet is suggested to help mitigate negative symptoms of a disease, aligns with intuitive eating because you are eating in a way that treats your body with respect and care. If a trusted, weight-neutral healthcare provider recommends a specific diet for your condition, know that choosing to follow it as a form of self-care and respect, as opposed to from a place of restriction, is intuitive eating.

It's Not Your Fault! Diets Don't Work!

If your TV stopped working, would you blame yourself or expect a replacement? I'm going to go out on a limb here and assume you'd take no fault and ask for your money back. Yet what happens when you go on a diet and the diet doesn't work the way it was promised? If you're like most people, you blame yourself.

The diet industry is a $72 billion industry for a reason: People are constantly buying into the promise of a better life with a diet. If solid scientific evidence proved that a diet safely and effectively led to sustained weight loss, there wouldn't be so many diets. There wouldn't need to be so much confusion and shame wrapped up in eating, either.

There's a reason diets don't work: Your body is biologically determined to keep you alive, especially when it comes to keeping you safe from famine. This means your body does everything in its power, both physically and psychologically, to protect you from losing weight.

Your body sees any sort of restriction as famine, and it'll do all it can to reverse weight loss. So, regaining the weight you lost on diets is completely normal. In fact, most diets do not result in long-term weight loss, and most studies claiming long-term weight loss only show statistics from up to five years, which is hardly a lifetime.

Diets typically boil down to the same advice of eating fewer calories (energy input) than you burn (energy output) in a day to create a deficit. Theoretically, this deficit leads to weight loss. However, energy input and output are a lot more complex. This intricate system is regulated on multiple levels. Most notably, a decrease in calories causes your body to naturally respond by stimulating hunger *and* reducing your metabolism.

A 2016 study published in *Obesity* followed contestants from the popular reality show *The Biggest Loser* and found that after losing weight, the body has metabolic adaptations that cause a decrease in energy burned at rest. This happened even after the contestants returned to their original weight or ended at a higher weight than when they started the show. Separate studies published by P. S. MacLean and F. L. Greenway showed that weight loss caused significant decreases in the hunger-suppressing hormones leptin, cholecystokinin, peptide YY, insulin, and amylin. It also led to an increase in ghrelin, the hunger-stimulating hormone, plus an increase in participants' subjective appetite.

Study after study shows that the body adapts by becoming more efficient in protecting you against weight loss, otherwise known as famine to your body. Your body acclimates to these new levels of energy intake and expenditure after weight loss. Not only that, but various studies, including a 2011 study published in the *Journal of Applied Physiology*, show that both calorie restriction and weight loss led to decreased energy burn during physical activity. Meaning if you lost weight, then participated in the same activity as someone of your new size, you would burn fewer calories when exercising (as well as at rest) than they would. And, according to the other studies previously mentioned, you'd also feel hungrier because of the change in hunger and fullness hormone levels.

Furthermore, the mind feels deprived by the decrease in calories or food groups and notices this unmet need of nourishment. In turn, the mind starts seeking what it can't have, which typically causes uncontrollable eating. Research shows that self-imposed deprivation increases the excitement, feeling of reward, and motivation to obtain the restricted food.

It's no wonder diets don't work! Ultimately, diets take you away from trusting yourself. They strip away your autonomy over your body. Diets steer your attention to your outward appearance instead of encouraging you to turn inward to really understand how to nourish your body. The following sections describe a few common diets and why they typically do not work.

Low-Calorie Diet

Most diets involve calorie restriction of some kind because cutting calories theoretically leads to weight loss. A low-calorie diet can be highly restrictive and negatively alter your metabolism. Such diets often provide the bare minimum of calories your body needs to function at rest. They do not take into account your genetics, lifestyle, or other factors, so you might be eating significantly less than your body really needs each day. This can lead to weight loss, yet it also decreases your resting metabolic rate, which requires you to eat even fewer calories to maintain that weight.

Low-calorie diets require a bit of planning and prep to ensure you are not consuming more than the prescribed number of calories per day. This can lead to decreased mental health and feelings of guilt or failure if you continually consume more than the diet recommends. It is also difficult to meet your vitamin and mineral needs with a low-calorie diet, which can also cause fatigue, brain fog, preoccupation with food, cravings, nausea, constipation, diarrhea, gallstones, irritability, and muscle cramps. Furthermore, food restrictions often result in missing important life events or connections with loved ones.

Ketogenic Diet (Keto)

Despite its recent gain in popularity, the ketogenic diet has been around for a century. It was originally intended for children diagnosed with epilepsy to reduce the frequency of uncontrollable seizures. The keto diet involves eating a diet high in fat and very low in carbohydrates, so your body breaks down dietary fat into ketones. Your brain's preferred source of energy is carbohydrates, so it takes a lot of effort to switch your body to using ketone bodies as fuel. This can be physically and mentally taxing, which can make it very difficult to sustain a keto lifestyle. Plus, the safety of following the keto diet long term is not well documented.

One following the keto diet must consume 20 to 50 grams of carbohydrates per day, and mostly fat, which is highly restrictive. For example, if you were aiming to only consume 20 grams of carbohydrates, one small apple would hit your quota. You'd be left only consuming meat, fish, poultry, cheese, and oils. Fruit, vegetables, beans, nuts, seeds, and nearly everything else all has carbohydrates. Because grains, starchy vegetables, and many fruits are higher in carbohydrates, the keto diet can make it challenging to get enough fiber, vitamins, and minerals if you do not take special care planning your diet to include these necessary nutrients.

The keto diet is expensive and time-consuming to plan and prepare foods. Some side effects of the keto diet include bad breath, digestive issues, and poor bone health. People on this diet also experience the "keto flu," which is flu-like symptoms that arise while your body becomes accustomed to using ketone bodies as fuel. These symptoms include nausea, vomiting, diarrhea, constipation, fatigue, lack of focus, muscle cramps, irritability, cravings, headaches, and dizziness.

Like all low-carbohydrate diets, it is common for those who strictly follow the keto diet to lose a large amount of weight. However, many people find that drastically limiting carbohydrates often leads to bingeing. After stopping the diet, it is almost impossible to prevent weight regain.

Atkins

Like the keto diet, Atkins is a low-carbohydrate diet. In Atkins, you start with a very limited amount of net carbohydrates, about 20 grams. Then you increase your intake to up to 100 grams of carbohydrates per day. Net carbohydrates are calculated by subtracting the amount of fiber from the total carbohydrates.

Although you will not track calories, you will track carbohydrate intake. Tracking carbohydrates can be cumbersome and frustrating when you realize how limited your options are with such a small amount. Along with other low-carbohydrate diets, Atkins has similar downsides like bad breath, digestive issues, potential for nutrient deficiencies, and flu-like symptoms at the beginning of the diet.

Because it is so restrictive and typically expensive, Atkins can be very difficult to adhere to long term. The Atkins company has a product line to help extend your food options, but these products can taste like bland imitations of foods you truly love. In addition, weight loss resulting from the Atkins diet or any other low-carbohydrate diet is usually reversed when you stop restricting carbohydrates. If you ever decide to enjoy freshly baked bread, you'll likely regain weight faster than you can say "goodbye, Atkins."

Paleo Diet and Whole30

The Paleo Diet website states that when you follow this diet, "you are eating the optimal foods for your body, literally programmed into your DNA." While the Paleo Diet does promote consumption of foods like those our ancestors ate, it is hard to substantiate claims that suggest eating foods that are "programmed" into our DNA is significantly advantageous. Most research showing the benefits of this diet studied the eating habits of only a small group of people.

This diet goes by many names, including the caveman diet, Paleo Diet, primitive diet, stone-age diet, and Whole30. It is based on eating foods that our ancestors might have eaten during the hunter-gatherer era. While each diet differs slightly, potatoes, grains, legumes, dairy, sugar, and processed foods are typically eliminated. Often this diet is labeled as a lifestyle, yet there is still a focus on weight loss and eliminating foods.

This diet is usually nutritionally balanced, but it can feel very limiting. Plus, many of the foods recommended on the diet are expensive, and preparation of meals can be time-consuming. Accessibility to fresh produce, meats, and other ingredients could be another factor in making this restrictive diet unsustainable.

Furthermore, humans are no longer in the Paleolithic era. Thanks to modern inventions, you can enjoy delicious foods like bread and cheese. If these foods do not make your body feel nourished, it is fine to skip them. However, feeling guilty because you are not eating the foods your ancestors theoretically ate is not good for your mental health. In fact, anxiety around food can lead to bingeing or physical discomfort.

Intermittent Fasting

Intermittent fasting is restricting the *times* you eat instead of the amount or type of food you eat. There are different ratios for how long to fast and when it is acceptable to eat depending on the information you use regarding intermittent fasting. Common fasting ratios are 16-hour fasts with an 8-hour eating window, or eating normally for 5 days and severely restricting for 2 days.

Many people enjoy intermittent fasting because there are no restrictions on *what* you can eat, and there are some potential health benefits of intermittent fasting. However, intermittent fasting does not allow you to honor your hunger levels outside of the eating window, which can cause fatigue, lightheadedness, preoccupation with food, moodiness, and cravings.

Another issue with intermittent fasting is that it does not encourage gentle nutrition. It can also be restrictive if you plan to attend functions that involve eating when you should be fasting. Restriction can also lead to powerlessness around food and eating excessive amounts.

Macro Counting

When counting macros, you track what you eat to ensure your intake matches designated requirements for the day. Although this tracking can feel less limiting than counting calories or omitting food groups entirely, it is still restrictive. Tracking what you eat and making sure it fits into what is "right" or "wrong" can be anxiety-provoking.

Weighing and tracking foods can be time-consuming and labor-intensive, especially in the beginning when you are trying to figure out the correct ratio of macronutrients for your body. When only focusing on consuming the specific macronutrients of carbohydrates, protein, and fat, you could potentially miss out on getting enough micronutrients like vitamins and minerals.

Weight Watchers

Weight Watchers uses a proprietary points-based system for foods and gives participants a specific number of points they can consume in a day. This program is one of the most studied diets, and it does have research to support its claims of sustainable weight loss. The catch is that you must continue to restrict yourself to a set number of points every day, and you must continue to stay on the Weight Watchers diet if you want to maintain your weight loss. Another downside is that it can cause you to become preoccupied with tracking and manipulating your intake based on points.

In the end, it's important to remember that Weight Watchers is a business, and for a business to be successful, it needs continual income. If the program was truly successful in teaching you a sustainable lifestyle that gave you the freedom to eat what your body really wanted and needed, you would not need to continue Weight Watchers.

Weight Watchers has recently rebranded itself WW to attract more clients who are interested in "wellness" instead of weight loss. However, the company continues to glorify weight loss. And any plan that promotes weight loss is, in fact, a diet.

Nutrisystem and Jenny Craig

A meal delivery diet is nice because it is incredibly convenient. Almost all the food is prepared and sent straight to your door, which can be great if you are busy. However, it is expensive and doesn't do much to teach you about the type of foods that feel good in your body. Nor does it encourage gentle nutrition, because you are simply opening and consuming whatever you were sent. The processed foods on meal delivery diets might also make you feel deprived, as the food can be lacking in flavor and visual appeal.

These diets can be difficult to stick with because you are limited to the delivered foods, in addition to fruit, low-fat dairy, and nuts. Moreover, while there are many options for food, the variety could potentially lose its appeal after a few months on the diet.

HMR Program and Slim Fast

Meal replacement diets like the HMR (Health Management Resources) Program and Slim Fast are incredibly restrictive. Generally, you are instructed to eat one full meal, usually dinner, and replace the other meals with shakes. Exercise is encouraged, and some plans help you transition from the meal replacement to eating a low-calorie diet after the weight is lost. However, a low-calorie diet must be continued to sustain any weight loss.

These diets can feel very depriving, and with only about three flavors of meal replacement shakes, you might easily get bored. As with all low-calorie and low-fat diets, the restriction and lack of substantial, satisfying meals make this diet incredibly difficult to sustain and could lead to disordered eating habits.

Low-Fat Diet

Low-fat diets were all the rage in the 1980s and '90s, and supporters believed eating less fat meant less fat on your body. We now know this is highly oversimplified, yet low-fat diets are still suggested in some health conditions as well as touted for promotion of heart health.

Some research supports the low-fat diet as a good alternative for certain health conditions, but it can feel restricting. Contrary to popular belief, fat is an essential nutrient. Limiting it can cause you to have vitamin deficiencies, because certain vitamins are fat-soluble and need fat to be absorbed in your body. Plus, fat is beneficial for skin and brain health. Furthermore, a low-fat diet might lead you to avoid nutritious foods high in health-promoting fats like salmon and avocados. Dietary fat also helps you feel full longer, so reducing it could limit satisfaction at meals.

A common habit of people on a low-fat diet is to replace snack foods that are higher in fat with low-fat snack foods. The low-fat snacks often lack the flavor of the original version, so people tend to consume larger amounts of the diet food or binge on other foods to distract themselves from a craving.

The Yo-Yo Effect

Most people go on multiple diets, so their weight fluctuates often. Want to know the wild part? *Going on a diet is a predictor of weight gain.* You start a diet with the intention to lose weight. However, you end up gaining weight back and lowering your metabolism. Studies show most people return to their original weight within 1 or 2 years, and many often end with a weight higher than where they started. This is called weight cycling or yo-yo dieting, and this can be *worse* for your health than staying at a higher weight.

The repeated loss of weight and subsequent regain in weight cycling is due to the metabolic shifts in your body that favor weight regain after weight loss. Your body prefers to remain at a stable weight—your set-point weight range—so it does everything it can to return you to your starting weight or bring it even higher.

Multiple studies connect weight cycling directly to compromised physical and mental health. Weight cycling is associated with higher total mortality, increased risk of hypertension, coronary heart disease, cardiovascular disease and inflammation, greater weight gain with an increase in fat mass higher than what was originally on your body, and loss of lean muscle mass.

There are also many negative side effects to one's psychological health, including life dissatisfaction and greater emotional distress, in addition to less physical activity and a higher prevalence of binge eating. The most notable part? Weight cycling increases risks of developing the aforementioned diseases to a greater extent than remaining the same weight, even in people considered "obese."

Wellness Is a Trap

Say hello to the ultimate charlatan: wellness. Yes, wellness is great in theory: Adopting self-care practices, making nourishing food choices, increasing daily movement, and implementing helpful stress management strategies are all wonderful things. However, the wellness world portrayed on social media is filled with farmers' markets, boutique exercise classes, and luxurious yoga retreats that are not accessible to everyone. It makes true wellness, or the act of feeling well in mind, body, and spirit, seem unattainable for most people. Wellness culture convinces you that your current lifestyle is bad, wrong, or unhealthy, and it guilts you into making changes. Messages like "it's not a diet, it's a lifestyle" or "food is medicine" cast judgment and imply your lifestyle and food choices are inferior. You are constantly sent messages that you are not good enough.

The message of self-improvement in the name of health can make you feel the need to always be doing more. Your behaviors around eating, exercising, and taking care of yourself can all be negatively impacted by the wellness industry. For example, it can cause you to feel anxiety around eating certain types of foods. Or maybe you work in an area without easy access to nourishing foods, and the wellness industry makes you feel guilty for eating processed food for lunch. Or maybe you must decide between going to a yoga class or spending time with your family.

Wellness culture implies that if you are not eating perfectly, exercising regularly, or meditating daily, you are not healthy. But you may have neither the resources nor the desire to achieve perfect health. However you decide to pursue health is ultimately up to you. Don't let the wellness industry trick you into thinking you need to prove your worth through your health and appearance.

Diets in Disguise

The wellness industry is full of diets in disguise. Anything that encourages you to limit foods to specific amounts, types, or times is a diet, as well as anything that encourages changing your body for weight loss. Clean eating, juice cleanses, and detoxes are all diets. Anything outside of yourself that tells you what, when, or how to eat is a diet. Even when something claims to be a lifestyle change and not a diet, it's still a diet if it attaches morality to food. (I'm looking at you, clean eating and Whole30.)

These devious diets make you feel guilty for eating certain foods. For example, clean eating has very moralistic undertones. Are you dirty if you aren't eating "clean"? Not only do they make you feel guilty for not eating perfectly, these clever tactics also make you think your body isn't properly working and needs to be fixed. If you have functioning kidneys, lungs, and a liver, your body is already detoxing for you.

Please don't feel bad if you've fallen into these traps. Sometimes I let these messages get into my head, and I've been practicing intuitive eating for more than five years. No one is immune to diet culture's tricks. However, unlike those fake "boost your immune system and win at life" pills, you can build up the strength to fight these diets in disguise.

At the end of the day, any diet or lifestyle plan will give you a false sense of hope for an improved life simply by following a set of rules. In truth, it is just taking you away from your body.

Social Media and Its Hidden Effects

Who knew little square photos could affect your life so much? Social media has undoubtedly transformed the way you interact with others, measure yourself, and view life. It can be both wonderful and incredibly problematic.

Social media is great for connecting with others you don't regularly see, but it can also shine a light on all the ways you feel you aren't measuring up to others or your own potential. Photos on social media can feed your feelings of inadequacy, and studies show all this can lead to feelings of guilt and body checking.

A significant amount of research associates social media use with lower self-esteem, negative body image, higher desire for a thinner body, disordered eating behaviors, and higher internalization of the thin ideal. Many influencers and celebrities on social media have straight-sized bodies (that is, *they fit into small through large clothing sizes*). Seeing these bodies to the exclusion of other bodies can spark feelings of inferiority and make you hyper-aware of your appearance.

Social media can make you question the value of your own body and life. It's exhausting! How can you consciously navigate social media in a way that honors your mental health? Here are a few tips:

» Turn off notifications.

» Mute or unfollow any accounts that make you feel bad about yourself.

» Diversify your feed. Follow positive accounts.

» Scroll with a realistic and compassionate lens. Remember your values, so when you see something that makes you feel jealous or inadequate, you don't forget what is important to you.

» Set time limits in the app.

» Nurture real-life relationships. We need human connection.

The Comparison Mindset

Social media invites comparison even when it presents so-called #reallife images. Using social media as a measuring stick for your life is not productive. It can cause you to be more self-critical.

Luckily, you can give yourself a dose of self-compassion to fight the comparison trap. According to Homan, et al., "Individuals high in self-compassion are mindful, kind, and nurturing toward themselves during situations that threaten their adequacy, while recognizing that being imperfect is part of 'being human.'" Kristin Neff, a lead researcher in self-compassion, states, "Self-compassion entails treating oneself with kindness, recognizing one's shared humanity, and being mindful when considering negative aspects of oneself . . . self-compassion does not entail self-evaluation or comparisons with others. Rather, it is a kind, connected, and clear-sighted way of relating to ourselves even in instances of failure, perceived inadequacy, and imperfection." Self-compassion can reduce the negative effects we feel when we start to compare.

Put It Into Practice

Self-compassion is a skill that will benefit you on this entire journey. You might find it especially helpful when it comes to social media. Next time you go on social media, try applying the three components of self-compassion.

SELF-KINDNESS:

» How can you be kind to yourself when you are using social media?

» What can you do to be more accepting of yourself?

COMMON HUMANITY:

» Everyone feels inadequate sometimes, and most people are only posting photos of the positive things in their life.

» Remember that social media is a highlight reel, not an accurate depiction of everyday life.

MINDFULNESS:

» Before logging onto social media, consider why you are turning to it right now. What do you want to feel in this moment?

» Pay attention to how you are feeling while on social media. What caused you to feel this way? What truths can you remind yourself so you don't get stuck ruminating over the negative feelings from social media? Example: "Instagram is a highlight reel, and no one shares the bad stuff. Everyone has insecurities, too. I'm a good person, and my life is no less valuable than theirs even if they can afford to travel all over the world."

Conclusion

Your body wants to keep you safe, and weight loss feels unsafe to your body. Focusing on weight loss and changing your body may not benefit your life, and it can actually cause a great deal of harm. Remember that instead of fighting your body, you can treat it with compassion and implement health-promoting behaviors to improve your well-being.

You now know why diets don't work and some of the ways diet culture can sneak messages that we aren't good enough into our lives. In the next chapter, you will learn about reconnecting with your hunger and fullness signals. Good riddance to the diet mentality. It's time to eat!

CHAPTER 3

Reconnecting with Hunger and Fullness

Now that you are familiar with the principles of intuitive

eating
and have a better understanding of why many diets can be
unhealthy and hard to sustain, you will look inward to start the
recovery process. To begin, you'll reconnect with the sensations
of hunger, fullness, and pleasure. You'll learn about

» Types of hunger and what causes you to feel each of them

» Differences between emotional hunger and physical hunger

» Methods to kindly and effectively cope with your feelings

» Ways to achieve satisfaction in eating

» Practices to reconnect to feelings of hunger and fullness in your
   body

» The Hunger Scale and how to use it

Through each eating experience, you can discover what brings
satisfaction, fullness, energy, and focus. The great thing about your
body is that you can learn so much from feelings of hunger and
fullness, and these sensations help you know how to meet your
needs.

We Were Born Intuitive Eaters!

Generally, babies cry when they are hungry and stop when they are
full. They make it seem so simple, don't they? Truth be told, we are

all born with these innate hunger and fullness cues. Intuitive eating comes to us naturally; our ability to use it has simply been worn down by the messages that claim our body is untrustworthy and not good enough.

In childhood, we learn that food is more than simply nourishment, and we begin to start interacting with it differently. Offering food as a reward, insisting that all the broccoli must be eaten, or demanding a clean plate before we can be excused from the table can confuse how we relate to food. Additionally, we connect with people through food, so food is associated with community and love.

It's not our caregivers' fault that we are no longer intuitive eaters. We are all doing the best we can, especially around food. Luckily, intuitive eating allows us to appreciate both the physical and emotional aspects of food without the conditions diet culture places on food.

To return to our natural-born intuitive eating habits, it takes some unlearning of certain behaviors. Using the intuitive eating framework, you will relearn how to use your own internal wisdom to feed your body by honoring hunger and feeling fullness. You will learn how to meet your physical and emotional needs with compassion and care. You will learn how to trust your body again.

Honoring Hunger

Feeling hunger is a good thing. It is simply your body's signal that it's time for nourishment. Your body tells you what it needs if you only listen. One of the best things you can do to rebuild trust in your body is honor your hunger by feeding your body when it asks for food.

There are so many factors that affect the intensity of hunger you feel, including sleep schedule, amount of daily activity, illness or injury, menstrual cycle, medical conditions, stress levels, and even the weather. Hunger levels change daily, and it is normal to want different quantities of food at different times. If you've dieted, you might be used to eating the same amount of food. You might feel out of control when you finally allow yourself to honor your hunger. Know that your hunger levels are strictly related to your body's needs and nothing else.

When relearning to honor hunger, it's helpful to consider the type of hunger you are experiencing. I like to separate hunger into four types that relate to the thought, emotion, and instinctual facets of intuitive eating:

» Physical hunger

» Practical hunger

» Sensory hunger

» Emotional hunger

Physical hunger is a normal biological cue. When your stomach is empty, it secretes hunger-stimulating hormones, like ghrelin, that tell your brain, "I need food." Once your stomach has what it needs, your pancreas and intestines release appetite-suppressing hormones like cholecystokinin, polypeptide YY, and insulin. These hormones travel in your bloodstream to your brain to tell your hypothalamus, "Thank you; I'm good with food for now."

With **practical hunger**, you use the knowledge you've gathered in the past to know when you might not feel physically hungry, but you need to eat. Maybe you're not ready to eat lunch, but you have meetings for the next four hours. If you wait to eat until after your busy day, you'll be a hungry monster. Therefore, you decide to eat something now, even in the absence of hunger. Another example is when you have no appetite because you feel sick, but you know you need to nourish your body with food.

Sensory hunger is when you are motivated to eat based on the appearance, smells, sound, touch, and taste of food. This type of hunger can be tricky, so call on your satisfaction skills to aid you when experiencing hunger from your senses. When you eat in the absence of hunger because something tastes or looks good, remember that it is not satisfying to eat past fullness, and it will be significantly more enjoyable if you wait until you are hungry. If you have unconditional permission to eat, you will always be allowed the food, so there's no need to eat significantly past fullness even if it looks good.

The last type of hunger is **emotional hunger**, which usually gets labeled the bad apple of hunger. Emotional hunger is reaching for food in reaction to your feelings as opposed to having physical sensations of hunger. Despite what diet culture suggests, emotional eating is not something to "overcome." Instead, emphasizing the importance of meeting your needs to the best of your ability will help you cope with your emotions with kindness.

Overall, remember that hunger and the ways it shows up in your body are normal. If you're not accustomed to listening to hunger signals, the sensation of hunger can trigger many reactions in you, like frustration and anxiety. Or you may feel that your hunger signifies that you are more self-disciplined because you did not eat past fullness. However, hunger does not give any insight into the type of person you are. Hunger is meant to be an emotionally neutral experience.

The Effects of Restriction

The negative effects of restricting what you eat are numerous. Restriction can lead to a decreased metabolism as well as muscle loss. Other physical symptoms of restriction include extreme fatigue, anemia, interrupted sleep, hair loss, skin conditions like acne and hyperpigmentation, digestive issues, fertility challenges, and poor bone density. The mental health effects of restriction and deprivation are cravings, increased desire to eat when not hungry, depression, avoidance and fear of foods, decreased satisfaction of appetite, eating past fullness, unrestrained eating, dependence on palatable foods to cope with uncomfortable emotions, and preoccupying thoughts about food, weight, and body shape.

Physical vs. Emotional Hunger

After years of stifling sensations of hunger and fearing the onslaught of emotional eating, it could feel daunting to truly honor hunger of any type. Don't forget that all hunger is valid, and it might not always be satisfied with food. In intuitive eating, you show respect for your body by listening to it and honoring its needs.

The difference between hunger types is the *reasons* they present themselves. Physical hunger is your body alerting you it needs more energy to function. Emotional hunger is your body warning you that you have an unmet need. Practical hunger is knowing you need to eat despite the lack of physical hunger, and sensory hunger is feeling the desire to eat because one of your five senses was triggered into wanting food.

Being able to differentiate the type of hunger you're experiencing allows you to truly meet your needs. If your body is physically hungry, yet you try to satisfy this hunger by calling a friend, you're going to end up even hungrier. Likewise, if you try to immediately placate an uncomfortable feeling by eating, you will only numb the emotion, which will not leave you feeling balanced and comforted.

Recognizing Which Is Which

The beauty of recognizing what is going on every time you eat is that you get to learn a little more about your hunger and fullness signals. Start by understanding how each hunger type shows up in your body. Remember that physical and emotional hunger will differ from each other, and everyone's bodies are different.

Physical hunger is felt physically. The sensation typically builds over time, and eating any food satisfies physical hunger. Physical hunger is usually experienced hours after a satisfying, filling meal.

Emotional hunger can appear at any time and doesn't depend on when you last ate. It appears when your needs aren't being met and is usually precipitated by an emotion. Every emotional feeling has a physical sensation, and food alone does not typically satisfy this hunger.

Coping with Emotional Eating

Sadness, boredom, loneliness, disconnection, anxiety, emptiness, excitement, and anger can lead to emotional hunger, which can present as negative thoughts, cravings, painful sensations, or the absence of physical hunger.

The actual emotions you feel are not wrong, but the challenge lies in how you respond to the emotions. To help you accurately respond to emotions, you need a toolbox full of ideas on how to cope. Moreover, you must know what your needs are, and how to satisfy those needs. Without coping mechanisms outside of eating, you might consistently turn to food when another activity could make you feel better. If your needs are not being met, it will make understanding and coping with your emotions a lot harder.

Start by noticing what emotion you are feeling and how it is showing up in your body. How intense is the emotion? How and where are you experiencing the emotion in your body? Next, analyze and reframe the thoughts you are having regarding this emotion using a nonjudgmental lens. Finally, decide how you will respond to the emotion based on the intensity of the emotion you are feeling.

It's okay if you sometimes use food to soothe. It's okay if you misunderstand the emotions you are feeling or how to best serve yourself in the moment. It's okay if you have trouble figuring out what you are really hungry for at the moment. Know that as you continue this practice, you will become more skilled in accurately identifying your emotions and meeting your needs.

Put It Into Practice

Get to know your emotions. When you find yourself emotionally hungry, not physically hungry, take this opportunity to acquaint yourself with the emotion. The next time you feel an emotion that causes you to reach for food, try working with your emotion through these three steps:

» Label the emotion you are feeling and the intensity of it.

» Reframe the situation. Notice any alternative ways to view what's happening.

» Choose a response or coping mechanism to deal with the emotion.

FOR EXAMPLE:

» **Label:** You're outraged that a coworker ate your sandwich. Your shoulders are tight, and you're so upset you can barely talk.

» **Reframe:** Instead of yelling "My sandwich!" at your coworker or eating anything you can find, you get your coworker to buy you lunch at a new restaurant close to the office.

» **Choose a response:** While waiting for lunch, you distract yourself by watching a funny TV show.

Navigating Stress and Food

Whether it causes us to crave or avoid foods, stress can greatly impact your eating habits and relationship with food. However, you don't have to be a willing bystander in your body's reaction to stress, and managing stress lessens its impact on how you eat and relate to food.

Stress eating is a typical response to trying to regulate stress. However, consistent stress eating may cause feelings of guilt, which only makes things worse. Studies show stress can also create unnatural hunger and cause people to crave more palatable foods like sugar and fat. Whether stress causes you to have uncontrollable cravings or to feel nauseous thinking about food, neither is wrong.

First, not taking care of yourself will make eating a lot more challenging. If you do not care for yourself or do not manage your stress, food becomes even more important and more rewarding.

If you don't have a clue on how to reduce stress, it's time to come up with some coping mechanisms. Some examples of stress relievers are to take a nap, meditate, move your body, color, talk to a therapist, listen to music, write a letter, or read. This is where the coping toolbox comes into play.

Regular mealtimes can also be helpful in managing stress because routines help you feel grounded and stable. It is also nice to know that you are still taking care of yourself by continuing to nourish your body with food. This is very important if certain stressors cause you to avoid or forget food.

Give yourself the space to honor the stress but not to push it away by mindlessly eating. If you always use food to cope with stress, you will likely have a strained relationship with food. Instead of using only food to manage anxiety, you can use an idea from your toolbox of coping mechanisms.

Put It Into Practice

Create a toolbox of coping ideas to help you more effectively deal with feelings. Not every idea in your toolbox is going to fit every situation, so it's helpful to have multiple choices. Write down some ideas for each group so you have options to pick from next time you have a strong feeling.

» **How will you directly process your feelings?** Example: Write in a journal or talk to a therapist.

» **How will you distract yourself?** Example: Watch TV or read a book.

» **What types of support from others would feel helpful?** Example: Ask a friend for help or talk to a family member.

» **How will you allow the emotion to be instead of suppressing it?** Example: Meditate or call a friend to vent.

» **What self-care activity will help you feel cared for?** Example: Cook for yourself or spend time in nature.

» **What mood boosters will make you feel better?** Example: Play with a pet or volunteer.

If you try something and it doesn't help, don't feel bad. Instead, try another option. This is a learning experience, so remind yourself that next time, a different tool could be a better fit for this specific situation. For instance, I know that when I feel sad, I can deal directly with my feelings by journaling or calling a friend for support. However, distracting myself with TV or social media does not usually alleviate that stressor.

Distracted Eating

Ever finish a meal and have almost no recollection of what you just ate? This is distracted eating, and it can greatly interfere with your ability to notice what's going on in your body. There's no need to feel guilty when this happens. However, it's hard to listen to your body if you're distracted. Countless studies show that when distracted, people continue eating beyond the point at which they reach physical fullness, and I believe it's hard to feel satisfied if you barely taste or acknowledge your food.

When you are not paying attention to how food tastes and how it feels in your body, you aren't able to fully appreciate the food and the act of eating. Distracted eating is all too common, and it's a difficult habit to stop completely. However, there are a few things you can do to help decrease distracted eating and get back to enjoying food and connecting with the eating experience.

Pause. A pause allows you to make a conscious choice. It empowers you to make the decision that is best for you in this moment. Pausing can be done before you eat, during your meal, and after. Before the meal, decide what you want to eat. How do you want the food to taste? What textures, temperatures, and smells do you want? How can you make this experience comfortable and peaceful? After the meal, examine how your body feels from the choices you made. Bonus: The insight you've gained from pausing will help you make more satisfying choices in the future.

Set up obstacles to mindless eating. Distractions happen, but it's possible to set up obstacles to keep distractions from causing you to miss out on engaging with and enjoying your food. Mindlessly eating from a box, carton, or bag leaves you feeling guilt for eating the whole thing without noticing. While there is no shame in eating the whole thing, you might feel frustrated and defeated after missing out on your hunger and fullness cues. Instead, try putting the food on a plate or in a bowl to give yourself a physical cue to pause.

Check in. Check in midway through the eating experience. What does your food taste like? What are the textures and smells? Is it satisfying your hunger? Would something else taste better? Do you need more of something? Do you want to continue eating? There's no wrong answer. Checking in allows you to make a choice during the eating experience, instead of not realizing you're full until your hand hits the bottom of an empty bowl.

Enjoy one meal per day without distractions. Having one meal each day where you completely focus on eating and connect to your food will lead to more enjoyment. Turn off the TV, silence your phone, and shut down your computer. Pay attention to how the food tastes and how it feels in your body. There's no need to do this for every single meal, but allow yourself to enjoy at least one distraction-free meal per day. This gives you a chance to savor your food and honor your hunger.

Seeking Satisfaction

Satisfaction is key in helping you connect to food. Rediscovering the pleasure from food is one of the main perks of intuitive eating. Plus, feeling satisfied helps you more easily notice hunger and fullness cues. Feeling satisfied feels like wholeness. After polling some of my friends, many of them described satisfaction as being comfortable, full, and happy. The feeling of satisfaction you get from something you've enjoyed eating makes you feel full, with no desire to eat more —even if a plate of loaded nachos is in front of you. When you feel satisfied, you might notice feeling energized, nourished, focused, content, and in a better mood.

When you're ready to eat, consider the foods you have available that bring you joy. What amount of this type of food do you need to eat to satisfy your hunger? What would help you feel your best at this time? For instance, I love cheese and crackers, but they would not be satisfying for dinner. However, I could add pear slices, salami, walnuts, and bread, and that would be a satisfying meal with enough energy and substance.

When selecting a meal to satisfy hunger, try to include foods that offer a combination of carbohydrates, protein, fat, produce, and fluid.

For example, chicken and vegetable noodle soup sprinkled with cheese. Or a tofu stir-fry served over rice with a glass of iced tea and a cookie. It's okay if the meal doesn't include everything, but it's a helpful guideline to ensure you get enough energy and an array of nutrients in your meal.

To create a satisfying experience with food, it helps to eat in a peaceful environment. It can be difficult to feel satisfied if you feel anxious about food, if someone you're dining with discusses how "sinful" food is, or if others judge your food choices. While it is not always possible to eat in a pleasant atmosphere, try to do what you can to decrease the stress of the meal.

Finally, not every meal is going to be satisfying, and that's okay. Sometimes your only option isn't very exciting. There's no shame in not feeling completely satisfied after every single meal. Thanks to intuitive eating, you know that some meals will be amazing, some will be average, and some will be uninspiring, and all of it is okay.

The Hunger Scale

From absolutely ravenous to so full you cannot breathe, and everything in between, hunger and fullness signals can tell you so much about your body. However, after years of ignoring hunger and fearing fullness, it might be challenging to decipher these cues. To aid you in befriending your hunger and fullness sensations, try using the Hunger Scale.

When you first start eating intuitively, consider the sensations listed on the scale that relate to hunger. Later, when you are more attuned to your personal fullness levels, you can adjust the scale to fit your cues. Here is an example as a starting point:

HUNGER SCALE

1: Starving, extreme physical discomfort, sick, lightheaded, must eat now

2: Very hungry, so hungry you could eat this guidebook

3: Meal hungry, stomach growling, food looks really good right now

4: Snack hungry, starting to notice signs of hunger, feeling a little fatigue

5: Neither hungry nor full, comfortable

6: Hunger is gone but not quite satisfied

7: Satisfied, not hungry, not overly full, pleasant fullness

8: A smidge too full, zero hunger signs

9: Not even a little bit hungry, uncomfortably full

10: Extreme physical discomfort, bloated, nausea, the thought of eating feels terrible

How to Use the Scale

The Hunger Scale doesn't need to be rigid. It's merely a guide to help gauge whether you are physically hungry and what your body needs at the time. Some questions to ask yourself when using the Hunger Scale:

» What does it feel like in your body to be incredibly hungry?

» What does it feel like to be hungry or a little bit hungry?

» What does it feel like when you are comfortably full or satisfied?

» What does it feel like to eat past fullness?

Because children are naturally intuitive eaters, I enlisted the help of some of my favorite kids aged 10 and under to give me their signals to know when they were hungry and full. I included their comments along with ranges for using the scale.

1–2: At this point, you are so hungry that you will eat absolutely anything. Your primal hunger instinct kicks in, and you are more likely to eat quickly and to eat past fullness.

"My stomach tells me to feed it right now!" "My stomach feels sick." "Angry stomach."

3–4: You are hungry enough to eat a meal or snack but not too hungry. This is a good place to be when you eat because it is easier to listen to your hunger and fullness cues. If you are meal hungry, make sure to eat a larger meal. If you are slightly hungry, a snack might be sufficient.

"Stomach feels empty." "My stomach keeps getting my attention."

5: Food feels unimportant right now. You are neither hungry nor full. This typically is experienced about an hour after eating a meal, when food is off your mind.

"I don't think about food at all."

6–7: In this range, you are getting to a place where your body would be okay to stop eating. You might start to notice signs of fullness and signs of satisfaction, both mentally and physically.

"Thank you for dinner, Mom and Dad, can I go play?" "My stomach feels happy."

8–10: You've eaten past hunger in this range. It's not bad to eat more than you physically need, but you might want to explore the reasons for eating past hunger if it happens often. It could be caused by distracted eating, emotional or stress eating, or waiting until you are overly hungry to eat.

"Can't look at food anymore." "Hard to move my body."

Breaking the Habit

Creating new habits is not easy; it takes time and effort. But it's worth the time and effort to relearn how to eat intuitively. This won't be a quick fix, so be patient. If you punish yourself for your eating habits or ruminate over the choices you make, remember to show yourself some compassion. Allow yourself to explore how different types of hunger show up in your body, to learn from your eating habits, to discover new ways to meet your needs, and to ultimately connect to your body's hunger and fullness sensations.

According to a 2010 study in the *European Journal of Social Psychology*, it can take more than two months to implement a new habit and to break unhelpful patterns. Remember that you are already an intuitive eater. You are simply working on making that intuitive eater your decision maker instead of letting the food police and diet culture rule your life. Every time you challenge negative thoughts or make choices that meet your needs, you are one step closer. Each challenge teaches you something new. Keep going and remember that there is no way to fail at intuitive eating!

Fullness Cues

Paying attention to your fullness cues can be confusing at first, and it can also bring up uncomfortable feelings. You might feel guilty for feeling "too full" or assume that fullness means you ate too much.

Remember that recognizing and honoring fullness takes time and practice. Fullness is a normal, neutral biological cue. It's as boring as your appetite-suppressing hormones sending messages to your brain that your stomach has received adequate energy. Paying attention to physical fullness feelings is the fun part, and it is strictly about connecting with your body. It has absolutely nothing to do with your worth or willpower.

The first step to recognizing fullness is decoupling any feelings of morality from sensations of fullness. Confront any rules around fullness you might still practice. Were you taught to clean your plate as a child? This could contribute to feeling the need to eat everything on your plate even when you aren't hungry. Do you limit amounts of specific foods? You might not be eating enough if you control how much food you are allowed to eat. At any point in your life, did you experience deprivation from diets, caregiver restriction, or food insecurity? Deprivation can cause you to binge on foods you fear you won't be able to eat for a long time.

While there are many examples of how food rules tamper with your ability to recognize fullness, it's important to remove the power these rules have over your eating. After you've removed morality from hunger cues, you can get to know what fullness feels like in your body. There's no wrong or right way to feel your fullness, and your body already knows what to do. It's up to you to eliminate the food rules and conditions you place on eating, so you can bring out your natural intuitive-eating self.

Remember that intuitive eating is not the "hunger-fullness diet." You are free to eat whenever and however much you want. It is up to you to decide when to stop, and for the most satisfying experience, it typically feels best to stop when you are comfortably full.

How Dieting Can Interfere with Your Fullness Cues

Diets train you to eat only specific amounts or types of foods, which completely confuses your internal fullness signals. Want cheese? "Only one ounce." Beans? "They're good for the heart but just eat a little because of the carbs." And forget about eating that afternoon snack. "You're not hungry; you're just bored. Chew some gum or drink a big glass of water. If that doesn't work, try lighting a scented candle or go for a walk."

Consider how these suggestions would apply to needing to use the restroom, another normal biological cue in our body. Think of how ludicrous it would be to chew gum, drink a big glass of water, light a candle, or go for a walk when you just needed to go to the bathroom! When you intently listen to your body—not food rules—you can learn what true hunger and thirst feel like in your body.

Food policing thoughts from diet culture lead you to lose the connection you have in deciphering hunger and fullness. Ditching the diet mentality and any food rules are integral in making the connection to hunger and fullness cues. Without these connections, you'll never be able to truly trust your body to get what it needs and eat intuitively.

Reconnecting with Your Fullness Cues

Every time you experience hunger and fullness cues, you can learn a little more about your body. Paying attention to eating is essential to reconnecting to your hunger and fullness cues. Our bodies just want a little attention.

Take note before, during, and after eating to see what might be happening in your body. And always remember that there is no right or wrong way to do this.

Putting together all you've learned so far, use these prompts to reconnect to your cues next time you eat:

» **Consider how hungry you are.** Think about the foods available to you in this moment and how much you would need to satisfy your hunger. What foods and amounts will help you feel nourished, energized, revitalized, or whatever else you'd like to feel after eating?

» Midway through the meal, **pause and check in.** Is this enough food? Is this satisfying? Does it taste good? Adjust as needed.

» Once you've finished eating, **note how you feel.** Pay attention to physical sensations. Figure out whether you are satisfied, still hungry, or overly full.

Know that you don't have to analyze hunger and fullness levels every single time you eat. This is simply a helpful tool to bring these sensations to the forefront of your eating experience, rather than treating them as an afterthought.

There is no limit to how long you can spend learning your body's cues. Eventually, you'll get to a place where you will honor hunger and feel fullness without as much effort or stress, and you will be able to trust your body's internal wisdom without imposing external rules.

Conclusion

Satisfaction with foods is more easily found when you are the sole decision maker of the foods you eat and you do not use external rules to make these choices. With a clear understanding of hunger and fullness cues, you are better equipped to make sure your needs are met, which is essential to your well-being and managing your emotions. Remember that it takes time to reconnect to your hunger and fullness sensations, but each time you eat and learn from your experiences, you get closer to understanding your body. You're more than halfway there, and you've learned so much already. Take a moment to celebrate that. Now that you have a better understanding of hunger and fullness, you will work to restore your relationship with food and movement.

CHAPTER 4

A Recovered Relationship with Food and Movement

After discussing hunger and fullness and how to reconnect with these sensations, it's time to work on rebuilding a nourishing relationship with food and movement. You'll learn about

» Making peace with food

» Allowing yourself unconditional permission with all foods

» Changing your language for food and eating

» The importance of nutrition

» Making movement a part of your life no matter what body you have

This chapter focuses on creating habits that will satisfy your body and mind.

Calling a Truce with Food

Do you feel like you are in a constant battle with food? You might feel like you're either one bite away from disaster or one bite closer to perfect health. In reality, what you eat does *not* determine your worth or status. Though nutrition does contribute to your health, it isn't the only aspect of your well-being. Making peace with food, the third principle of intuitive eating, will help you get to a place where you no longer stress about food.

Despite popular opinion, food conditions or rules do not keep you safe. Instead, they keep you stuck. Making peace with food allows you to feel free and confident around food. Placing restrictions on food in any way will cause feelings of anxiety, obsession, and loss of control. Experiencing these feelings around food is no way to live. Food is meant to be a pleasurable way to nourish your body and help keep you alive.

An important aspect of making peace with food is unconditional permission to eat. Yet if you never give yourself this gift, it will be impossible to eat intuitively. Therefore, the third principle of intuitive eating is one of the most important steps in this journey. Allowing yourself freedom to enjoy all foods in any amount, at any time will remove so much unnecessary anxiety.

To start, examine any sort of conditions or beliefs you have around food that hinder your ability to make peace with it. Examples include limiting types of foods, "watching" what you eat, demonizing foods, and eating only at specific times. The problem with such beliefs is they rob you of your internal wisdom to make choices that serve your body best.

Food rules can cause internal friction when you are trying to allow yourself unrestricted permission to eat all foods in any situation. Even a simple rule like you "don't eat after 9 p.m." can be too limiting. Therefore, it's helpful to examine the beliefs you have around how you should eat and challenge them with facts. Instead of telling yourself what you cannot do, tell yourself, "I need to eat when I feel hungry. Some days, I might not eat enough earlier in the day to satisfy my hunger, so I feel hungry later than I usually do. Some days my body requires more than usual. That's okay and normal. My body is telling me what it needs, and it is up to me to meet those needs."

No More Demonizing Foods

Labeling foods as unhealthy, bad, or fattening is ever-present. You might use these words to describe certain foods sometimes, too.

This messaging is everywhere, from food packaging to billboards. What is *actually* unhealthy is attaching morality to foods.

It's easier to sell diets and lifestyle plans if people are scared to eat the "wrong" foods. Understandably, you don't want to eat something bad for yourself, especially when you are presented with evidence regarding how "toxic" a certain food is. But unless the food is poisonous, rotten, or causes an anaphylactic reaction in your body, it is not toxic. This statement even applies to sugar.

Because it's hard to allow yourself permission to eat everything if you are still fearful of specific foods, let me share some science-based information to help debunk the myths you've heard around specific foods. These facts are meant to help you stop fearing foods and to grant you permission to eat them if you want. Whether you eat certain foods is up to you.

Sugar

Many sugar haters share convincing evidence that sugar is addictive. They claim this because sugar consumption lights up the same pleasure center in your brain that cocaine does. You know what else lights up this part of your brain? Listening to music or seeing a friend smile.

Most scientific research on sugar addiction is done on *deprived* rats. As you've probably experienced, when you feel deprived, you are more prone to eat excessively. The release of dopamine in the brain when consuming sugar is *directly related to the amount of restriction*. Only the rats with restricted access exhibited addiction-like behaviors. One 2012 paper in the journal of the Institute for Laboratory Animal Research (*ILAR Journal*) noted that having restricted access to foods can "provoke excessive intake due to the uncertainty associated with opportunities to consume the palatable food."

The solution? Don't restrict your sugar intake. While sugar might not offer tons of nutritional benefits, it makes foods taste good, stabilizes foods, and allows us to connect to others through foods sweetened by sugar. And though sugar intake is associated with certain health conditions, it does not cause them. Certainly, it would be detrimental for sugar to be eaten all day, every day, but allowing yourself permission to eat sugar-containing foods without restriction means you decide for yourself when and how much feels good and what doesn't.

Fruit

The first time I heard someone tell me they couldn't eat bananas because they had too much sugar, I almost choked on my grapes. Ugh, diet culture!

Yes, fruit has sugar. It is naturally occurring sugar, and there is more of it in fruit than in most vegetables. But the tired platitudes that sugar is addictive or causes diseases has been debunked. Plus, fruit offers benefits like fiber, vitamins, minerals, phytochemicals, and antioxidants that help fight diseases in your body. While eating fruit, you're less likely to feel the common sensations people experience, like a drastic drop in energy, when consuming sugar-sweetened foods. The fiber in fruits also helps keep your blood sugar more stable.

There's no need to limit the amount of fruit you eat because a diet bans them or limits you to a small amount. Eat the types of fruit you enjoy in the amount that feels right for you.

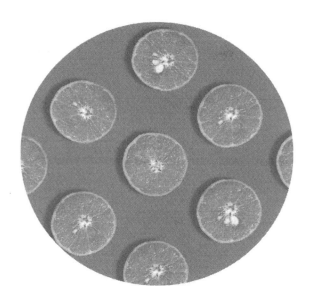

Gluten

Gluten is a group of proteins found in wheat, barley, and rye. It's also found in many different types of food thanks to its stabilization powers. Those diagnosed with celiac disease, a wheat allergy, non-celiac gluten sensitivity, or other related conditions understandably need to avoid gluten. However, the general population need not fear it.

Much of the research condemning gluten, including a 2017 study published in the *BMJ*, regards people with a preexisting sensitivity to gluten, so it makes sense that gluten would cause negative effects like inflammation and digestive discomfort in this group. However, in people without such sensitivities, studies show insignificant evidence of whether gluten is the cause of these issues.

I was once convinced I had a sensitivity to gluten because of the uncomfortable feelings I had when consuming gluten-containing foods. Once I allowed myself permission to eat foods with gluten, I realized I tended to overconsume them. I had been restricting myself, eventually overeating, then feeling guilty and uncomfortable.

The anxiety I felt and my tendency to binge on these foods were the real culprit.

My experience is not meant to shame or invalidate anyone who feels discomfort when eating gluten or any other food, nor did I share it to undermine the seriousness of celiac disease and other gluten-sensitivity conditions. I shared my own experience with gluten to show how anxiety and fearmongering around food can cause physical discomfort in your body, which can lead you to believe that you have a sensitivity to something.

If you allow yourself *full* permission to eat a food yet choose not to eat it for personal reasons or because it does not feel good to your body, it means you are practicing intuitive eating. It's all about making food choices based on what works in your body and being attuned to it, rather than fearing foods.

Pay attention to how you label food. Even if you aren't ready to eat certain foods, consider how you can change the language you use around food to be more neutral. Altering how you think and speak about food improves your relationship to food.

You Aren't What You Eat

"You are what you eat" is quite the judgmental phrase. This highly inaccurate statement assumes that our health status is directly caused by what we eat. You are not guaranteed to lead a life free of illness simply because of the food you eat.

What you eat does *not* define you. You're not gross for eating half a dozen donuts or bad for eating chicken wings for dinner. Whether you eat takeout and packaged foods or organic produce and home-cooked meals, your value as a person is no different.

To move away from this mentality, notice what foods make you feel guilty. Next time you eat one of them, give yourself a reality check. Did you steal the food? Did you hurt someone to get this

72

food? Are you breaking any laws? No? Well, then you are not "bad" for eating it.

I realize it isn't so easy to change the way you think about yourself when it comes to food. It will be an ongoing evolution. Just as you are altering your language regarding food, you need to update the words you use to describe yourself and the way you eat. It can be accomplished only by changing your perspective and reframing your thoughts. You deserve to eat without excuses or conditions. Most important, your value is *not* attached to the food you eat.

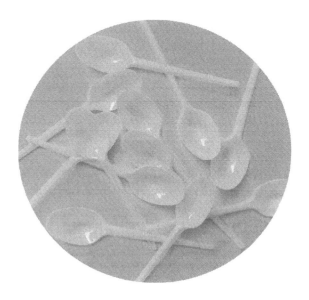

Put It Into Practice

Challenge your unhelpful beliefs, especially when labeling how and what you eat. Analyze your thoughts about the way you eat. Carefully consider what is true and what might be false.

Instead of thinking: I should eat more vegetables. It's bad I didn't have one yesterday. I'm so unhealthy.

Try thinking: Vegetables are nourishing for my body, but it's okay if I don't eat five servings every day. My body cares about the averages of my intake. When I'm not worried about what I'm eating, I am less stressed and it's easier to get a variety of foods. Eating a variety of foods and managing stress are both health-promoting. I'll make a conscious effort to eat two vegetables tomorrow.

Instead of listening to what diet culture tells you, listen to what your body tells you it needs. Honor those needs and what your body wants.

Eating Without Penance

Making peace with food means you have complete and total permission to eat whatever, whenever, and however much. Any time you eat a specific food or amount with the condition that you will "make up for it," you are punishing yourself for eating. For example, you only eat a salad for lunch to "save" for a restaurant dinner. Or you force yourself to exercise 30 minutes longer because of the muffin you ate at breakfast. Such acts of conditional eating remove much of the pleasure around food.

Making up for what you ate or saving calories for later means you will never be able to fully enjoy food. Instead of spending life in food purgatory, work toward eating without penance. Allow yourself the freedom to eat without adding points to the next day or promising to exercise more or restrict later.

Permission without conditions makes food emotionally neutral. This shifts you away from seeing certain foods as forbidden—foods that you want but can't have—or *can* have, but at a cost, like disease or higher body weight. These are challenging thoughts to overcome, but years of diet culture's stigma on food, health, and weight must be undone. As you embrace intuitive eating, you'll slowly work to make food less emotionally charged. You can still feel excited about eating your favorite foods, but you no longer feel guilty or the yearning to eat in excess.

To make a food less emotionally charged, you must always have access to it. You need to train yourself to know that it is *always* an option, so you will no longer have the drive to binge from the feeling of limited access to the forbidden food. Making food emotionally neutral allows you to feel at peace with food.

Put It Into Practice

To make peace with food, you must give yourself the permission to eat all foods, in any amount, without conditions. Habituation is helpful when working on this principle. This is allowing yourself to eat a formerly forbidden food repeatedly, so it no longer becomes so emotionally charged. Here's how to start:

» **Select one food.** Use the same brand and flavor each time.

» **Decide where, when, and how you will eat this food without distractions.** What do you need to feel secure? Make sure you are not in a vulnerable spot and you are not overly hungry.

» **Eat the food without distractions.** Truly taste it. Take pauses while eating to see how you feel physically and mentally. Keep reminding yourself as you eat that this food is always available.

» **Repeat until you have conditioned yourself to know that the food is no longer banned.** When you no longer worry about having limited access to this food, you will be less likely to eat it uncontrollably.

Nutrition Is Necessary

One of the biggest pushbacks to intuitive eating is that people assume health is completely ignored. On the contrary, intuitive eating is centered on health. Unlike most diets or lifestyles, intuitive eating highlights beneficial behaviors that promote good health, independent of weight.

As a registered dietitian nutritionist, I love sharing how nutrition and food are important to our well-being. Yet it can be difficult to decipher health-promoting behaviors from those inspired by diet culture. For that reason, I recommend waiting to incorporate the principle of gentle nutrition once you have made peace with food and are able to respect your body.

Eating nourishing food gives your body energy, satisfies hunger, improves mood, and helps you focus. Choosing a variety of foods gives your body an array of nutrients. Carbohydrates provide your body with energy and aid in digestion. Fruits and vegetables are high in phytochemicals, which are related to decreased prevalence of chronic conditions like diabetes, cardiovascular disease, and cancer. Protein builds and repairs muscle, and fat helps absorb nutrients and facilitates essential functions in your body.

When you start to incorporate gentle nutrition into intuitive eating, it's helpful to understand what foods feel good in your body. Instead of trying to eat only the most nutrient-dense food possible, find what healthy means to you, as it means something different to each person. For example, a handful of almonds provides a nice balance of protein, fiber, and nurturing fats. You'll also get a hefty dose of vitamin E, manganese, and magnesium. For someone with severe tree nut allergies, however, almonds must be avoided.

Focus on getting a balance of nutrients that help you feel your best. Nutrition is important, but it's best to consider the big picture as opposed to individual meals and foods. Define what healthy food means for you. What foods make you feel physically good? Find the foods that feel nourishing to you and eat them often.

Reading Nutrition Labels Productively

Nutrition facts can be helpful if you take a gentle nutrition approach to understanding the information. You might have previously used nutrition information to determine what you can and cannot eat or how much you are allowed to have according to food rules or a diet. However, intuitive eating uses nutrition labels as neutral information, and nothing more.

When you first start implementing intuitive eating in your life, I recommend ignoring the nutrition facts on foods because they can be distracting. The exception would be for food allergies and sensitivities where you need to ensure a food is allergen-free. Once you feel like you are attuned to your body's needs and give yourself unconditional permission to eat, you can explore using nutrition labels to assist you when eating.

Knowing the nutrition facts of food can help you understand what feels good in your body. After you've explored what helps you feel energized and satisfied during a meal, you might notice you need at least a certain number of calories in a meal to feel satisfied to prevent undereating. Everyone has different needs, which is why it is so important to explore what works best for you. Another way nutrition info can be helpful is if you are trying to eat more of a specific nutrient like fiber to promote digestive health. The nutrition facts can help you determine whether you are eating the amount that feels best for your body.

Remember to use nutrition facts as a guide and approach the information with curiosity instead of judgment. It's not a "bad" meal if the ingredients don't contain a certain number of nutrients. Nutrition information is simply additional data, not a rule. These details should be used to complement your intuitive wisdom on what feels good in your body.

All About Balance

Balance in eating can feel impossible to achieve, but our body focuses on the big picture, not individual meals or days. If you don't eat a single fruit or vegetable for a few days, nothing dire will happen. Because we are striving to incorporate health-focused behaviors into our lifestyle, we can use our brain's wisdom to know that eating fruit and vegetables we like contributes to positive health. Try serving lettuce and salsa with tacos, or eat chocolate-covered strawberries for dessert.

By considering your taste buds *and* your body's cues, you can find balance in what you eat. Think about how eating candy and ice cream every night for dinner would not feel satisfying once you had experienced a stomachache after eating. But limiting yourself to eating only one type of food isn't going to be enjoyable either. When you consume a variety of foods you enjoy eating, you give your body and mind nourishment and balance.

Honoring Your Body with Food

When you become comfortable with your hunger, fullness, and satiety cues, you begin to understand what foods feel best in your body. Knowing that no foods are off-limits gives you the freedom to make decisions that respect your body, instead of rebelling against restriction or feeling out of control around certain foods. Even if you eat emotionally or in the absence of hunger, you can use your instincts to learn from the experience to honor your body in the future.

Making food choices from a place of self-care allows you to appreciate what feels good in your body, satisfies you in the moment, respects your values, and makes you feel energized, focused, and positive. Eating food you like sustains your mind, body, and spirit, which also helps you feel more attuned to meeting your needs in other areas of life. It helps build trust in your body. This kind of eating shows respect for yourself and repairs your relationship to your body.

Meal Planning and Grocery Shopping

When I was little, my mom made a weekly meal plan and posted it on the refrigerator, and we stuck to it. Me as an adult? I haven't made a meal plan in, well, ever. I'm the type of person who bases meals solely on the sales at the store that week. Whether you're like my mom, me, or somewhere in the middle, having some version of a meal plan can be a lifesaver to ensure you're adequately nurturing your body.

Some people assume intuitive eating and meal planning conflict; however, I think having at least a rough idea of what you want to eat helps make sure you're prepared. When meal planning, take note of your schedule, check the weather, and consider what's in season or on sale. But most important, be flexible.

Here are some things to consider when creating a dinner meal plan that includes a grocery trip: First, check your schedule for the week. Do you or your family have any activities, events, or trips planned? Are you in charge of cooking, or will you have help in the kitchen? Now, move on to the weather and what's in season. Soup is not going to sound all that appetizing when it's hot outside. What produce is in season? If it's the winter, tomatoes aren't going to be their best. Bonus tip: Seasonal produce is usually less expensive. While at the grocery store, check to see if there are any sales.

Now it's time to make the meal plan and shop. If you'll be busy later in the week, you can add a few slow cooker meals to your plan. Or grab frozen pizzas and bagged salad ingredients. Once you have the menu planned, make the grocery list and head to the store with a mentality that it is adaptable. For example, if you planned on beef tacos but you realize chicken is on sale, you could do chicken fajitas instead! In the same vein, if certain fresh fruits and vegetables aren't in season, frozen and canned are great options. If you have a roast planned for Tuesday but you decide to eat a casserole instead, that's okay. You can always switch up your meals for the week, and it's also nice to have a day to use up leftovers.

   As with intuitive eating, meal planning and grocery shopping are the most enjoyable when you leave room for flexibility.

Intuitive Eating on the Go

Intuitive eating is for all seasons of life. Know that there will be times or places that will not always provide you with a vast array of foods from which to choose. Luckily, intuitive eating isn't only about eating exactly what you want. Sometimes you just have a granola bar in your bag or a convenience store is your only option. Apply intuitive eating principles to these situations by answering the three questions for satisfaction:

  » What is available?
  » What sounds tasty?

» What will make me feel nourished?

For example, if you are at a convenience store and need lunch, start by looking through all the options and decide what sounds good. If possible, have a few ideas ready. What options will make you feel nourished, satisfied, and full? If you have a busy afternoon ahead, you don't want to feel lethargic. So only eating a bag of chips would probably not keep you full for long. Try adding sunflower seeds and an apple to go along with the chips. You get protein and fat from the sunflower seeds, fiber in the apple, and chips make your taste buds happy plus give you carbohydrates.

You can select foods that best fit these three questions, and that is intuitive eating. Anything goes as long as you allow yourself the freedom to base your available choices on what feels and tastes good.

Indulgence

If you've stopped restricting yourself, is there ever a need to indulge? In my opinion, no, because indulging implies that you'd be yielding to a desire or surrendering to a craving. Food no longer has power over you, so there's no need to succumb to it simply so you can enjoy some chocolate.

The term "indulgence" is a perfect example of how the language we use regarding food is so incredibly important. Changing how I described food was a huge turning point for me and when intuitive eating clicked into place. No longer referring to food as "healthy" or "guilt-free" altered the way I view the food I choose to eat.

Instead of referring to treats or rich foods as indulgent or fattening, try using descriptive words that do not attach morality to the food. When you use moralistic language, your mind views the food as good or bad. This can affect your perception of the food you eat, and you might internalize diet culture's ideals that you are "good" for eating certain foods and "bad" for eating others.

Doesn't a "warm, gooey chocolate chip cookie with creamy vanilla bean ice cream" sound more enjoyable than an "unhealthy cookie with indulgent ice cream"?

Movement for the Right Reasons

Many people consider movement as a means to change the way their body looks, to eat more, or to make up for something they ate. Yet intuitive eating is about adding health-enhancing behaviors to your life that have nothing to do with the way you look. Moving your body is beneficial for well-being, completely independent of your body size.

Intuitive movement is practiced as a form of self-care. It is moving the body you have right now, not focusing on a body you wish you had. Moving your body in ways you enjoy helps you connect to your body even more and enhances your ability to connect to satisfaction, hunger, and fullness cues. Moving your here-and-now body helps you accept and appreciate the body you live in. Adding movement into your life, regardless of your body size, will boost your mood, strengthen your body, and release stress.

Movement Gone Wrong

Sadly, incorporating movement into your life has been taken over by diet culture. Diet culture wants you to feel the need to change your body, so you will buy into an exercise program. However, if you move your body for the sole purpose of changing it, you will miss out on the plethora of benefits movement has to offer.

Our bodies are designed to move. But if the focus is on burning calories, losing weight, targeting "problem" areas, exercising past what feels good for you physically, or having an all-or-nothing mentality with exercise, you diminish the physical and mental benefits of movement.

Instead of thinking about moving your body to formally exercise, switch your mentality to adding bits of movement throughout your day. It's great to have an exercise routine if you enjoy it, but the benefits of movement aren't only relegated to exercising for a certain amount of time each week. Your body appreciates and thrives with all movement that feels good for you. Any movement is good if the intention is to enhance your well-being, not change your body size.

Benefits of Moving Your Body

There are numerous advantages to regularly moving your body that are not related to how your body looks. People who move their bodies have a lower prevalence of chronic diseases and typically live longer. Movement helps strengthen muscles and prevents muscle loss in aging. Exercise helps prevent osteoporosis later in life and reduces the risk of falling. For those with chronic pain, exercise can promote favorable effects in the reduction of pain severity as well as improved physical function.

According to a study published in the *Journal of Behavioral Medicine* in 2015, exercise improves sleep quality, time, and efficiency. Exercise also helps reduce fatigue, lowers triglycerides, and improves insulin sensitivity. Movement improves your sense of well-being and self-esteem along with boosting your energy. It leads to slower rates of age-related memory loss and cognitive decline. Furthermore, movement leads to fewer depressive and anxiety symptoms.

Trying New Things

Having a habit of moving your body is even better when you're doing something you enjoy. There are a multitude of options for moving your body, so it's a matter of finding what works best for you. Try different activities to learn what you enjoy. Search online for free workout videos to test different types of movement. If you have a park near your house, use the walking path or the equipment there. Who says an adult can't use the monkey bars?

Try activities you enjoyed as a kid or turn exercise into a social activity by meeting friends or your partner to exercise together. Do what you can to make these new experiences comfortable. Exercise with someone you trust. Go to places that do not promote body manipulation. Practice safety measures when exercising by yourself, like letting a family member know where you are walking and what time to expect you home. Wear clothes that feel pleasant and make it easy to move.

Whatever body you have, you need not be excluded from the option to move if you feel comfortable finding and participating in alternative forms of movement. However, it's important to honor what your body is capable of doing. For example, people with chronic pain or disabled bodies have a more limited range of options for moving. Please honor what you feel safe doing and what feels accessible to you. Nothing is too insignificant to be considered movement. Even simply stretching your neck from side to side can enhance joint mobility.

Tips to Turn Movement into a Habit

It's understandable if you feel anxious, overwhelmed, intimidated, or otherwise uncomfortable with the thought of adding exercise into your life. This is especially common if you've been shamed in the past for your ability or looks, or if you do not have safe access to places to move your body. Instead of feeling the need to join a gym or buy a bunch of new workout clothes, start small by adding movement into activities you already do. For example, walk around the office on a break, or meet friends for an exercise class instead of grabbing coffee (or do both). You can also stretch while watching TV, dance while dinner is cooking, or hop off the train or bus one or two stops earlier.

When it comes to a more formal exercise routine, doing activities you enjoy makes it easier to exercise on a regular basis. Removing barriers to exercise can also be helpful. Save a few workout videos on your phone and do them in your pajamas when you get out of bed. Make a playlist you are excited to listen to while exercising.

Do what makes you feel good; this behavior reinforces your enjoyment of movement. Take note of how you feel after moving. When I acknowledge how refreshed I feel after a walk, it makes it a lot easier to stop scrolling social media when I know a walk will help me feel better.

Don't forget that your body needs rest. It is not lazy or weak to rest. In fact, rest is as important as movement. You don't need to exercise every single day, and you don't need to feel guilty for watching TV without stretching. When you are connected to your body's needs, you'll be able to know when your body needs rest and when it craves movement.

Conclusion

You must allow yourself to eat freely to enjoy all foods and to reap the full benefits food provides for your body. Thinking of food in a neutral way helps you enjoy eating, too. Plus, making peace with food promotes emotional health, because health embodies many things and attaching your focus to one thing—food—can create problems. Without making peace with food, it will be difficult to truly nourish your body with gentle nutrition.

It's also important to shift your mindset and recognize that nutritional value isn't the only reason you make decisions around food. Intuitive eating encourages you to respect your needs and practice gentle nutrition by eating a wide variety of foods you enjoy and feel good in your body. Lastly, bodies are designed to move in some capacity. But remember to rest when your body needs it and only move when your body feels able.

CHAPTER 5

Recovering Your Self-Care and Self-Love

It's time to rebuild your self-worth and develop a healthy and loving relationship with yourself and your body. You'll learn how to

» Let go of the need to change your body to fit diet culture's unrealistic standards
» Grieve the loss of the time, money, and effort put into changing your body
» Set positive goals that do not revolve around weight loss
» Practice self-respect and supportive body positivity
» Implement true self-care into your life
» Trust your body
» Reach weight neutrality

We Have to Grieve to Move On

Ditching diet culture is not a one-and-done deal. So much of our existence is wrapped up in it that we cannot fully move on without grieving the loss of the life we were falsely promised. If we don't take the time to grieve, we cannot completely let go of all the damage diets have caused us. Grieving allows us to move on and create space, so we can be more fully present and live a life protected from diet culture's influence.

You may encounter different stages of grief in processing the sadness of leaving a diet culture–influenced life. You might experience denial when thinking diets aren't *that* bad, or you're trying to lose weight simply for your health. Anger can bubble up when you realize all the precious time you wasted and experiences you missed because of diets. Maybe you try bargaining by attempting one more diet to lose weight before starting intuitive eating. Furthermore, it's normal to feel sad when you realize you'll never have the ideal body or a life free from weight stigma.

You eventually will get to the final stage of acceptance, and acknowledge how dangerous diets are for your physical and mental health. You'll welcome intuitive eating as a way to heal from disordered eating and diet culture. Intuitive eating does not free you from all of diet culture's tactics, but your life will improve when you process the grief.

You must go through the muck to get to this place of acceptance; there's no way to just skip to this step. The body you have is yours for the rest of your life, and the relationship you have with yourself is undoubtedly the most important. To find a respectful relationship with yourself, you must say goodbye to the deceptive chase of the thin ideal, let go of the false sense of control, and mourn the loss of all the time, money, and effort you spent pursuing a smaller body. Grieve the lie you've been sold that told you that you need to fix your body. Your body does not need to be changed for you to be treated with respect and for you to feel worthy.

Goodbye to the Thin Ideal

Say good riddance to the illusive thin ideal. Halting your chase of the ideal body is a necessary step toward fully practicing intuitive eating. Respecting your body is impossible if you are constantly striving to change it. If you hold on to this idea of a dream body, you'll always be at war with your body and you will never completely embrace your life.

Pursuing what society deems the ideal body gives you the feeling that there is a potential to live life free from ridicule. It gives you the false sense of security that one day, if you simply try hard enough, you will no longer be punished for living in a body that doesn't meet cultural standards. When you are striving to have a thin body, you are working toward the common goal of toxic diet culture. Yet trying to achieve the ideal thin body will cost you your life. Not necessarily physically, but it will cause you to miss out on experiences, your true purpose, and a sense of peace.

This step is imperative, but it is not easy. It can feel challenging to let go of this dream because you know how difficult the world is for people with larger bodies, where bodies that are not thin are often vilified. If you've previously had a smaller body that felt easier to accept, it's okay to miss that body and the benefits that came along with it, like being able to eat without judgment from others.

Our society does not value larger bodies, which makes it even more difficult to allow yourself to be as you are. Acceptance can help you make room for the body you have and know that your old body was not better. Acceptance might bring up unpleasant feelings, but if you do not acknowledge them, you cannot release them.

Liberating yourself from the pressure to change your body takes you one step closer to body acceptance. Despite what people think, letting go of the thin ideal does not mean that you stop taking care of yourself. In fact, it's the opposite. Releasing the need to fix your body means that you allow yourself to be. You give yourself space to treat your body with care without trying to control it.

Goodbye to the Illusion of Control

Dieting or manipulating your food choices gives you a false sense of control. When you first make the switch from following diets to intuitive eating, you may feel frenzied. The more you try to control your feelings and choices, the worse it gets. The only way to feel harmony is to allow the chaos. Eventually you will be able to trust that your body will do what it needs to do.

The illusion of control over your body is that it helps you feel safe, but this is a bald-faced lie. Controlling your body does not bring you safety or peace. Think of all the times you tried restricting certain foods to be healthier or change your body, and you ended up eating uncontrollably as a result. Spoiler alert: You cannot control your life by controlling your body.

Letting go of this lie will allow you to feel at peace. It will strengthen the trust you have for your body. Plus, you can redirect your energy into doing things that truly improve your life, like taking care of yourself.

Goodbye to Time Wasted

Consider how much time you've spent thinking about food and manipulating your body. Reflect on the time wasted researching weight loss plans, fighting the urge to eat, excessively exercising, and more. It feels sad to realize how much time you spent worrying when you could have been connecting with others, experiencing the world, enjoying good food, pursuing your passions, or simply relaxing. But acknowledging the losses will make you realize that you'd rather have a more meaningful life instead of a smaller body.

The time you spent worrying about how you look can be spent now on much more worthy pursuits and experiences. A hike becomes more about appreciating the outdoors and taking in nature's beauty than burning calories. A trip to the beach is about relaxing and having fun with the people you love instead of worrying about how you look in a bathing suit. And a party is more about connecting with others instead of making sure not to eat the wrong things.

Setting Goals

Having clear goals inspires, excites, and motivates. Goals define the results you are looking to achieve and allow you to see your progress. However, goals are typically centered on body change.

Instead of setting goals based on external factors like weight or jean size, focus on goals in relation to behaviors that improve your quality of life. To help you set positive goals, highlight how you can implement the intuitive eating principles into your life. A helpful tool is the Intuitive Eating Scale (see here), which can help you pinpoint specific principles or practices you want to work on for setting goals. For example, if you strongly agree with the statement "I have forbidden foods that I don't allow myself to eat," you can refer to the section about eating without penance in chapter 4 to work on making peace with food.

Once you've decided on a goal to work toward, follow the SMART principle (see here) to define it. Then create a plan of implementation. You can set goals all day long, but implementation is the only way to achieve them. Your actions are what matters when it comes to reaching goals, so work toward increasing behaviors that enhance your life instead of diminish it.

Furthermore, it's important to be compassionate with yourself while working on your goals. Instead of using shame and judgment as negative motivators that cause guilt and procrastination, try a different approach. Research published in the *International Journal of Sport and Exercise Psychology* shows that "self-compassion is a significant predictor of self-determined motivation" and decreases self-handicapping. Self-compassion is a much more effective and positive method, as it helps you stay internally motivated while decreasing the chance that you will self-sabotage reaching your goals.

Stay SMART

It's hard to know when you achieve a goal if you simply say, "My goal is to be an intuitive eater." It's excellent you want to achieve that, but it doesn't give you much of a reference point, time frame, or specific method to reach this goal.

An alternative to creating such a broad goal is to apply the SMART characteristics to help you achieve and celebrate accomplishing your goal. SMART stands for setting Specific, Measurable, Achievable, Relevant, and Time-bound goals. In the example of trying to rid your life of forbidden foods, you can set a goal of, "I will feel more neutral about ice cream, my forbidden food, in six months. And I will keep it in the freezer at all times." This goal is specific, measurable, achievable, relevant, and time-bound, and it can help you decide what behaviors you'd like to add to your life to help you achieve it.

Be sure to allow some room for flexibility. You can always adjust your goals as needed. Negative pressure is not effective in reaching goals, so remember to use self-compassion as a positive motivator and to incorporate behaviors that improve your quality of life.

Words of Encouragement

Always remember that you are naturally an intuitive eater. You are simply doing this work to bring that instinct to the forefront as opposed to letting external influences make decisions about what's best for your body. However, this journey is not a straight line. You can't go from being a dieter striving to change their body to someone who exclusively listens to and respects their body's cues overnight. You will have both progress and setbacks when practicing intuitive eating.

As you work on incorporating more intuitive eating principles into your life, remember that it's a process and every little bit counts. Calling mashed potatoes "creamy and comforting" instead of "fattening," selecting the salad because you're craving veggies and not because you're trying to lose weight, and avoiding negative self-talk are all huge wins.

When you experience any challenges, and you most certainly will because you are human, reframe them as a learning experience. The good news is that there's no wagon to fall off or track to get back on in intuitive eating. Eating past fullness, feeling guilty for eating dessert, or distracted eating do not make you a failure at intuitive eating. These eating habits give you a chance to see what could have gone awry. Use each moment to boost trust in your body as proof that you are growing.

Practicing Self-Love and Body Positivity

Body positivity and self-love are essential to your intuitive eating journey, and they fall under the eighth intuitive eating principle: respecting your body. After so many years of diet culture's influence, it may seem impossible to go from disliking your body to an attitude of self-love and body positivity. But with patience and care, you can ease into this crucial mindset shift.

Body positivity as it relates to intuitive eating is knowing that your body is good no matter what it looks like. It is knowing that your body deserves respect no matter what its size is. Body positivity includes *all* bodies; there is no exception to the rule. Meanwhile, self-love doesn't mean self-absorption or selfishness. Self-love is compassionately caring for your body and meeting its needs.

Why are body acceptance and self-love important? Because they elevate your ability to tune into your body. Being in tune with your body allows you to practice intuitive eating with a clearer idea of how to serve your body's needs. If you are too busy critiquing your body, it is that much harder to listen to it. You cannot figure out what your body wants when you are preoccupied with making judgments about it. You cannot treat yourself poorly and expect to feel good.

The following 10 actions will help you develop more body acceptance and positivity. Note that some actions might resonate with you more than others. Take the ones you find helpful and leave the rest. Make them your own so they apply to your life.

Step Away from Tracking

Scales, step counters, point systems, and measuring tapes distract you from listening to your body. Measuring your body turns your focus outward instead of inward and prevents you from really tuning into your body's needs. Start by removing the scale from the bathroom and deleting food tracking apps from your phone. Even using clothing to judge your body size can be detrimental to body acceptance, and can weaken your ability to notice how you feel.

Instead of external tracking systems, start noticing your body's signals. You might even find it helpful to replace your tracking apps with notes that describe how certain foods make you feel or other sensations you learn from listening to your body.

Craft a Daily Self-Nurture Routine

Self-care is quite the buzzword in the wellness world, and many influencers flaunt their self-care activities on social media, making it seem like it is only for the rich and famous. However, self-care is not all manicures, massages, and vacations. It can be, of course, but self-care doesn't need to involve spending a bunch of money to treat yourself.

Reframe self-care to simply be activities you do to take care of yourself. Pick three to six things that you can do for yourself *every single day* that show your respect and care for your body—this is your self-nurture routine. Be sure to do these activities using a lens of self-respect and care instead of doing them because they are considered "healthy" or you are hoping they will lead to body change.

Some examples are making your bed, washing your face, brushing and flossing your teeth, wearing sunscreen, meditating, calling someone you love, journaling, eating a meal without distractions, stretching, and praying. The routine might already be something you do, but when you commit to doing these activities and showing up for yourself, you'll reap the benefits of self-care without the expensive price tag.

Thank Your Body

Think of one thing that your body helps you do and thank your body for it. Try to do this every morning or night because practicing gratitude for your body can help you appreciate it more. When you appreciate something, it is easier to respect it.

There are so many things your body does for you, even when it is not in perfect health. Your arms hug your loved ones, your reflexes save you from burning your hand when it's too close to the stove, your eyes see the sunset, your ears hear the birds sing, your lungs help you breathe, your hands text a friend, and your legs walk you up a mountain.

You have a body that fights day and night to keep you alive, and it deserves recognition. Thanking your body might feel cheesy at first. However, once you start acknowledging all the amazing things your body can do for you, you appreciate your body for its function instead of its aesthetics. A 2019 study published in *Body Image* showed that focusing on the functionality of your body can improve your well-being and body image. Your body is your home for life, so thank it for housing you.

List Your Accomplishments

Evaluate your life by something other than your body. Our bodies are meant to change, so if you want a stable self-worth, you cannot tie your value to a changing body. Even if you are happy with the way your body looks, placing all your worth in your appearance can result in pain on poor body-image days.

Acknowledging your inner and outer accomplishments gives you confidence that doesn't revolve around an ever-changing body. Write down your internal and external accomplishments and strengths. For example: setting healthy boundaries, volunteering, saying no to protect your mental health, running a 5K, being on time to work every day, loving your children, or creating a delicious cheese board. Accomplishments can be big or small. If you are struggling to come up with your strengths, consider the compliments you've received as well as your intelligence and talents at work or home.

Next time you struggle with feeling low self-worth because of your body, recall all your accomplishments and strengths that have nothing to do with the way you look.

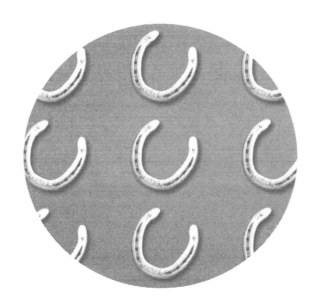

Post Encouraging Notes on Your Mirror

Write positive messages on notes to leave on your mirrors, refrigerator, doors, desk, or phone. Mirrors can be especially triggering to those who struggle with body image, so having a reminder that you are more than the way your body looks can be incredibly helpful.

Try to focus less on appearance and make the notes more about acceptance. Instead of, "Everyone is beautiful," which reinforces that beauty is important to our worth, use quotes like, "All bodies are good," "There is no wrong way to have a body," or "I am more than my body." Another favorite saying of mine is from researchers Lindsay and Lexie Kite of the *Beauty Redefined* blog, which says, "Your body is an instrument, not an ornament." These examples keep the messages positive yet accepting of all sizes.

Follow Social Media Accounts That Promote Body Respect and Diversity

Social media greatly affects our perception of beauty and body ideals. Following accounts that post before-and-after photos, calorie counts, or other triggering information can be harmful. Even "fitspiration" posts and photos meant to encourage physical activity and healthy eating can be problematic. According to one 2017 study in *Body Image*, fitspiration images and hashtags often reference or imply the need for self-control and discomfort to achieve goals and can therefore contain guilt-inducing messages.

Mute or unfollow any account that makes you feel bad. Do this no matter how likeable, relatable, or inspirational the person is. Instead, curate your social media feeds to have an array of accounts that support body diversity and body acceptance.

Seeing a variety of bodies expands your perception of beauty and shows how there are many different ways to have a body. It also highlights that beauty is not only on the outside but also in how the person displays kindness, self-respect, and care for others. If you find that your social media use is causing you to compare your body to others or is making you feel bad about yourself, consider setting daily time limits or taking a break altogether. Also, don't forget the self-compassion and social media exercise in <u>chapter 2</u>.

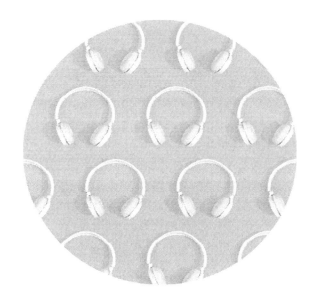

Create a Happy List and Treat Yourself Once a Week

Treating yourself is an important aspect of self-care, yet it looks different for everyone. You might love massages, and someone else would much rather go to the park with their dog. Sit down for a few minutes and write a list of all the things that make *you* happy. Maybe it's a weekly bubble bath, walk with a neighbor, video-chat with someone who lives far away, an hour to spend alone, or date night with your partner.

Schedule this time in your calendar and make it non-negotiable. Creating space for fun and pleasure is not only enjoyable, it's also beneficial for health by showing yourself that you are important and deserve to be treated well.

Wear Clothes That Feel Comfortable

Clothes are meant to fit your body, and not the other way around. Bodies are not intended to be forced to fit into certain clothes, and you are not meant to stay a specific body size or type your whole life. Forcing yourself to wear clothes that do not fit, whether they are too loose or too tight, does not show your body respect.

Donate, sell, trade, or alter clothes that no longer fit the body you have right now. Keeping clothes that previously fit you in hopes that you will one day fit into them again can cause you to hold onto the idea that your body needs to stay a specific size, and that is simply unrealistic.

The goal is to wear clothes that make you feel comfortable, whatever that means to you. When finding clothes for your current body, avoid the traps of wearing clothes based solely on size on the tag or how the clothing looks. Pay attention to how the clothing feels on your body, whether it gives you freedom to move without restraint, the sensation of the fabric, or whatever else you find appealing.

Compliment Others Without Commenting on Appearance

While this isn't exactly *self*-love, the way you compliment others is often related to what you value. If the compliments you give are based on the way someone looks, it shows that you admire appearance, which is normal and completely reasonable. However, appearance is likely not the only thing meaningful to you, yet we often compliment people only based on looks.

Start giving compliments that honor other qualities you see in people. Comment on the way someone's laugh always makes you smile, how they are excellent listeners, or how skilled they are at finding bargains. It doesn't need to be a deep, highly meaningful compliment. Any non-appearance compliments help you shift focus. Practicing this means noticing more than just appearance in others and yourself.

Move Your Body in a Way That Brings You Joy

For many, exercise is used to grant permission or as punishment for eating certain foods, and it is often coupled with body manipulation. Work on shifting this perception of exercise to an attitude of including joyful movement in your life because it feels good and promotes positive health.

When you immerse yourself in an activity without concern that it will change your body, you can really experience the beauty of movement. Moving your body in whatever capacity your body allows can be fun, plus it allows you to experience the strength of your body no matter what your abilities are.

Self-Care for the Sake of Self-Care

Taking care of yourself is one of the most important things you can do for your health and well-being. You are the only one who truly knows what you need, so you are the best one for the job to decide how to care for yourself. When you make choices from a place of care, you are better able to truly meet your needs.

Practicing self-care allows you to live life in alignment with what is important to you. For example, if heart disease runs in your family, you might value heart health. Therefore, you can strive to practice ways to protect your heart like meditating and praying to manage stress, incorporating movement regularly to strengthen your heart and improve its efficiency, and eating fruits and vegetables because they are associated with reduced risk of cardiovascular disease.

Instead of thinking that self-care is selfish, consider how you must take care of yourself to serve others. Just like on a plane when you are instructed to put on your oxygen mask first before helping someone else, you must do the same in real life. Because if you run out of oxygen, you can't help anyone.

Trusting Our Bodies

Our bodies are smart. They let us know when we need energy, sleep, fluid, movement, rest, connection, and more. Your body performs every moment of every single day to keep you alive. Even if your body isn't in peak health or ability, your body tirelessly works for you.

Traumatic experiences, years of mistrust, and insistence from diet culture that your body is unreliable all make it difficult to trust your body. Instead of assuming you will quickly start trusting your body or, alternatively, worrying it's impossible to rebuild that trust, notice the small ways in which your body proves it can be trusted. Some examples include how your skin forms a scab to heal from a cut, your heart beats faster when you are running to get your blood flowing, and you get goosebumps when you're cold to generate heat.

Eventually, you will notice your body working when you feel hunger pangs, signs of fullness, and awareness of emotions. This is all evidence of your body functioning and showing its trustworthiness. Pay attention, and let your body take care of you. Believe your body and use it to guide you in making decisions.

Put It Into Practice

Write a letter to your body. Expressing how you feel about your body helps you connect with it on a deeper level, and connection is the gateway to trust. When writing your letter, consider the following questions:

» How would you describe your relationship to your body?

» What are your challenges and strengths?

» What do you like and dislike about your body?

» What parts do you appreciate? What are you learning to accept?

» What ways does your body prove its trustworthiness?

» What promises do you have for your body?

Try to stay caring, gentle, and positive toward your body. It deserves love and respect not only from other people but from you, too.

Worthiness Is Unconditional

Your worthiness is inherent. It does not depend on your health status, how you eat, or how much you weigh. When you accept this truth, you are inspired to practice self-care, set clear boundaries, treat yourself with compassion, and accept your body.

It is not easy to internalize this truth if you think you are undeserving. It's common to feel stuck waiting for someone or something to qualify you. If you have trouble feeling worthy, remember that your body is good no matter what. You were born with value that never leaves.

To condition yourself into deeply knowing your worthiness, try recalling these affirmations:

All humans are born with the same value, and it doesn't go away.

I am worthy regardless of my body, food choices, or health status.

My worth is not situational or circumstantial. I am worthy no matter what.

Reaching Weight Neutrality

Living with a weight-focused mentality means you are delaying your life if you feel your body is not acceptable. It requires you to give your body over to diet culture instead of living. However, when you feel neutral about your body, you are no longer preoccupied with your appearance. This frees precious brain space so you can truly thrive.

Releasing the focus on weight is very difficult. Messaging that your weight is highly important, if not the most important factor, in health and well-being has bombarded you for years. But true well-being and health are *not* weight focused. Health and wellness are assessed by other factors like quality of life, cardiovascular measures, and social connectedness.

Here are a few ideas to help you shift your focus to a weight-neutral mindset:

Use "fat" as a descriptor, not an insult. Stop negatively reacting to or dismissing the word "fat." Fat is often used derogatorily, but it is simply a description like green or blue. When you dismiss someone who says, "I feel fat" with "You're not fat, you're strong" or something similar, you imply that fat is bad.

Leave weight and body size out of the equation. Interrupt your tendency to use someone's body to uplift or bash them. If you have opinions about someone, make it about their character or personality, not their appearance.

Allow your body to be. Let your body be as it is. Allow yourself to feel frustrated that it doesn't meet the ideal body standards *and* know that it is okay and normal. You do not need to prove your value.

Focus on caring, not measuring. When you measure, you lose sight of what's important. However, caring for yourself and others helps you focus on positive behaviors instead of the outcome of a specific weight.

Benefits of the Weight-Neutral Mindset

Research shows that focusing on a weight-neutral mindset instead of centering on weight has multiple benefits. Studies published in *Appetite* and the *Journal of Obesity* show that doing so leads to weight stabilization, along with decreased waist-to-hip ratio, cholesterol levels, and systolic blood pressure. Improved self-esteem, increased sensitivity and trust in the body's signals that regulate food intake, and decreased depression are also associated with the weight-neutral mindset.

In one of the aforementioned studies, participants who received weight-neutral education continued engaging in health-promoting behaviors, had higher fruit and vegetable intake, increased regular sustained physical activity, and had higher quality of life compared to those who focused on weight. These participants experienced less body dissatisfaction, less drive for thinness, less bulimia, less sensations of extreme hunger, and less restrictive eating and loss of control after breaking self-imposed restriction.

Letting Negative Thoughts Pass

Automatic negative thoughts around your body and food are highly common, especially in the beginning of intuitive eating. But you are not your thoughts. Notice these negative thoughts and reframe them with the truth. Otherwise, your negative thoughts will hinder your intuitive eating process.

You might have thoughts that you need to change your body, or thoughts that you are eating unhealthy, "sinful" foods too often. These thoughts can lead to actions like restricted eating, excessive exercise, and obsessive control over food choices. None of these activities will make you feel better, enhance your life, or improve your health. Instead of being discouraged, know it's normal to have these thoughts. Then work to challenge them.

Notice your negative thoughts. Acknowledge and label the thoughts, then challenge them. Don't allow your life to be dictated by this unhelpful negativity. Replace the thoughts with truths and positive alternatives.

For example, you want a cookie:

» **Thoughts:** I feel guilty. I feel like a failure for not having any willpower, and I'm worried that I'll eat too many cookies. Plus, cookies are bad for you.

» **Challenge the thoughts:** Am I really a bad person if I eat a cookie (or 10)? Isn't it bad for my mental health to spend so much time ruminating over eating a few cookies? Even if I eat 10 cookies today, am I going to get diabetes and cancer?

» **Truths:** No, I'm not bad for eating cookies. My food choices don't dictate my value. However, food anxiety causes unnecessary stress, and stress is detrimental to my health. Also, one meal does not determine my health status, so I will not get cancer if I eat 10 cookies today.

» **Alternatives:** I eat the cookie and realize I don't want another; the cookie didn't even taste that good. Or I ate the cookie and decided to have one more, but I remembered eating more than two would give me a stomachache. Because I know the cookies are always available, I don't feel the need to binge.

Continuing Your Practice

Living in line with your values instead of subscribing to diet culture's rules requires effort. It gets easier over time, but this practice must be ongoing to strengthen your resolve against diet culture. Intuitive eating doesn't happen overnight, and there is no wrong or right way to practice it. This process looks different for everyone.

All the suggestions in this book, including the 10 intuitive eating principles, are meant to be implemented in a way that works for you. The principles are not rules, so adapt the guidelines to fit your personality and life. Match your behaviors with what is important to you to establish lifelong, positive habits. And stick with it.

Take the good with the bad and remember that diets will take you away from your own internal wisdom. Diets will steal your experiences, time, money, and quality of life.

Consistency and Perseverance Are Key

Diet culture is relentless, and its messages can be oppressive. Intuitive eating requires commitment to the practice. Restriction and control can feel familiar and enticing compared to intuitive eating's lack of structure and unknown variables. But just because something is familiar doesn't make it good for you. If you don't continue to work on implementing intuitive eating, diet culture's messaging can draw you back to a life of controlling and restricting. Fortunately, intuitive eating gets easier over time.

Remember not to let challenges feel like failures and to reframe them as learning experiences. You are not weak if you get conned into starting a new workout to get "beach body ready." Maybe you felt insecure on social media or worried your body wasn't good enough. Or uncertainty with work led you to try controlling your body because it felt like the only way to control your life. Learn from the experience, and imagine what you can do differently next time. Also consider what you can do now to reassure yourself that it's normal to feel insecure and worried, but also know that trying to fix your body isn't going to solve your problems.

Reaching Out for Support

A support system of some kind can be helpful in continuing your intuitive eating practice. Having someone who can sympathize with the woes of diet culture and the constant pressure to change your body is key. A friend or family member who is supportive and open to your desire to be weight-neutral is beneficial, but this might not be easily available.

If you do not have a friend or family member you feel comfortable confiding in, try finding support online. There are intuitive eating groups you can join, or you can find online communities on social media to encourage you in this process. A certified intuitive eating counselor or HAES-aligned healthcare practitioner or therapist can be helpful if you have the resources and are looking for more structured support.

Conclusion

Allow yourself to grieve all you've lost because of diets; this practice helps you release and move past the pain. Not taking care of yourself will make listening to your body a lot more challenging, so it's imperative that you meet your needs. By practicing self-respect and care, you can support your body no matter how it looks or changes throughout your life.

Remember that you cannot trust your body if you are trying to control it, and distrust of your body will keep you trapped. After all, when you accept your body, you are more likely to respectfully treat it with kindness instead of dwelling on how it doesn't measure up to society's ideal body. The way you look is not a reflection of your character, and it does not determine whether you are worthy of love and acceptance. In the next chapter, you will learn how to cope with different situations that could hinder your intuitive eating practice as well as how to continue applying intuitive eating to your life.

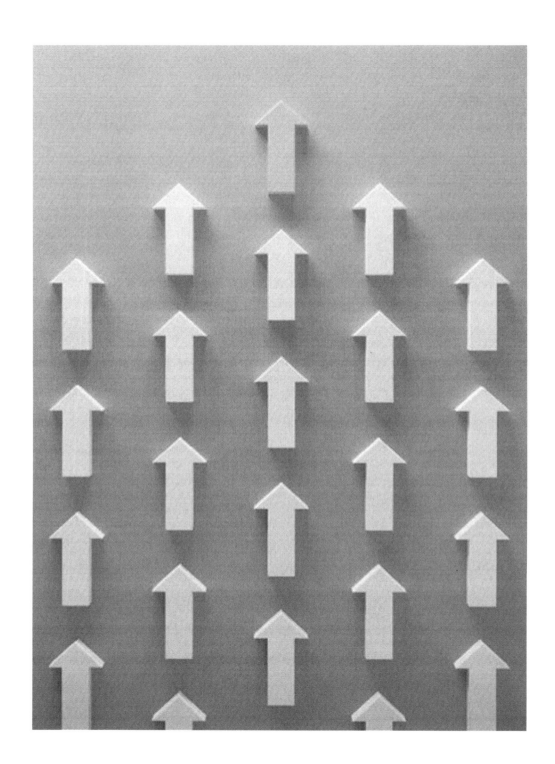

112

CHAPTER 6

Moving Forward and Allowing Yourself to Live Freely

Congrats! You've made it to the last chapter, where you'll finish getting set up for success in your intuitive eating journey. You'll learn how to

» Write a new body story celebrating the body you have

» Address potential body changes

» Prepare for possible triggering situations

» Draw healthy boundaries

Holistic Health

Whatever makes you feel whole and well—that's holistic health. It encompasses your whole self: body, mind, spirit, and emotions. Nurturing these facets can improve your well-being, and it is critical that you consider the big picture when striving to achieve optimum health. Focusing on overall health allows you to make space for all facets of yourself. Holistic health opens the door for you to explore health on your own terms, depending on your desire and abilities.

   Your bodily health is important to your well-being, but it's not the only factor. Just as you are not only a body, your well-being does not solely revolve around your physical health. Someone can be in poor physical health but have a high quality of life, and vice versa. Some bodies will never be physically healthy for many reasons, but that doesn't mean they should be left out of the health conversation.

Instead, center all areas of your health—physical, mental, emotional, and spiritual—to live in a way that works best for you.

Making Peace with Normalcy

You've been led to believe that having a "normal" weight, body, and eating habits are just on the other side of dedication, restriction, and control—and that changing your body will fix all your problems. This pursuit will make you miserable. You must let go of the idea of normalcy with your body, food choices, and health.

However, it's completely understandable to desire normalcy, especially if you feel like you are too much or not enough. Meeting the standard of normal provides protection from ridicule and feelings of unworthiness. If you stop trying to be normal, you risk being judged and shamed. Normal keeps you safe from substandard treatment, so your fears of never being normal are valid.

The problem is that trying to be normal results in a dull life. You stop doing things you love because you think you must postpone them until you have a normal body. You're so preoccupied with trying to shrink your body that you end up shrinking your life. You feel anxious, overwhelmed, and inadequate. Even if you achieve normalcy, you will still experience negative feelings toward your body and guilt about food choices if you do not confront the underlying issues.

Intuitive eating addresses the challenges we try to mask by manipulating our bodies. By working to make peace with food and learning to accept your body, you can release the need to be normal and take back your life. Don't let the attempt to have normalcy control you. Become an active part of your life instead.

Using outside influences as a guide prevents you from living a life true to yourself. It's doubtful you'd want to follow someone else's rules forever. To switch to following your own guidance, take the time to consider how you want your life to be.

To help you redefine yourself using your own wisdom, craft a new body story. To do that, imagine you were never told your body was wrong. Think about how you'd live if you weren't worrying about your body size or food choices. Finish by deciding how you'll implement these practices now.

Put It Into Practice

Write a new body story for the body you have right now. Instead of waiting for your body to change or letting outside rules define you, decide how you want to live in the body you currently have without letting it hold you back. When you are writing your new body story, consider the following questions:

» What would your days look like if you weren't focused on changing your body?

» How would you treat your body?

» What would you eat to nourish your body if you didn't worry about eating a certain way?

» What could you achieve if you weren't preoccupied with micromanaging your actions?

Once you have answered these questions, find ways to add these practices into your life. For example, if you noted that you would eat dessert, take the opportunity to figure out what desserts you love. Buy the ingredients or eat dessert when you're at your favorite restaurant. If you said you would do more activities that made your body feel good, replace some of your high-intensity exercise classes (which make you feel depleted) with more enjoyable, low-impact walks outside.

Basically, use these practices to show your body that it is important no matter how it looks or performs.

Addressing Potential Changes in Your Body and Weight

Intuitive eating helps you achieve your set point weight where your body feels its best. One of three things can happen in this journey: your weight can go up, go down, or stay the same. Unlike you've been conditioned to believe, your natural weight depends on genetics, not willpower.

You are not failing if you gain, lose, or have no change. All three options are normal. The purpose of previous chapters in this book is to help you accept yourself by appreciating your body's functionality and respecting it no matter what. Your body is designed to change throughout your life, and this can feel disruptive and highly upsetting if you attach your worth and success to how you look.

In a culture that values thinness and stigmatizes larger bodies, accepting weight changes can be one of the hardest parts of intuitive eating. Gaining weight might feel upsetting, and it's important to acknowledge this. Yet you can simultaneously know that your body is still good regardless of its size or ability. You might not like having a larger body at first, but try to allow yourself to just be. You deserve to take up space no matter how much space that is.

A growing body often makes others uncomfortable because of the stigma associated with larger bodies. However, someone else's comfort is not more important than your own life. Recall how much pain trying to shrink your body causes if you are tempted to be swayed by outside opinions. Don't forget how damaging it can be, both mentally and physically, to try to control your weight.

On the flip side, if you lose weight, people might praise your weight loss. Contrary to popular opinion, weight loss compliments are harmful because they place the accomplishment on someone's appearance instead of personal growth. Achievements such as listening to your body's cues, respecting your body, and kindly coping with emotions are overlooked because of the superficial focus on your body.

When you focus only on the way your body looks, you lose sight of how well you treated your body. Whether you gain weight or lose weight, remember how you've grown as a person instead.

Though you cannot change other people's judgments, you can modify your own. Start with compassion. Studies published in *Mindfulness* and *Psychology & Health* show that increased self-compassion is significantly associated with improvements in body dissatisfaction, body shame, body appreciation, and self-worth. Therefore, care for and treat yourself like you would a friend if they were upset. Think of the big picture, and remember that there are others experiencing this same stigma with weight change. And take a balanced view of the situation instead of letting your weight become your identity.

Reducing your own prejudice against larger bodies will also help minimize the impact of other people's opinions. What beliefs do you have about people with larger bodies? Your initial thoughts are your conditioned thoughts. Society has programmed you to measure worthiness based on body size, so it's not your fault you initially make these judgments. However, you can rewrite these thoughts and accept all bodies regardless of size.

Preparing for Potential Triggers

Not only are the media and healthcare systems telling you how to live healthily, your friends, family, and strangers are feeding you these messages, too. From weight loss ads to "guilt free" food labeling, the messages are everywhere. Unfortunately, these consistent, triggering messages around your body, eating habits, and health can be disruptive to recovering from restrictive or disordered eating.

Triggers can range from simple calorie counts on a menu to unsolicited, rude comments about your body. Anything that reminds you of a traumatic or negative experience can provoke a strong emotional response. Triggers cause your body to feel threatened even if a physical threat is not present, so you might feel anxiety, sadness, tension, powerlessness, or distress.

Triggers often produce feelings of shame, which causes us to feel unworthy. Shame can lead to reduced self-care, limited social interactions, avoidance of health care, and stress. Numerous studies, including ones published in *Child Psychiatry & Human Development* and the *Journal of Nervous and Mental Disease,* show that shame increases the risk of self-sabotage, drug and alcohol dependence, dangerous behaviors, and depression.

Rest assured that everyone has their own set of triggers, so becoming triggered is normal. Although unpleasant, experiencing triggers is not something to be ashamed of. You cannot rid these triggers from your life, but you can equip yourself to be ready for them. Holiday meals, doctor's offices, social events, and work/school stress are some of the most common triggering situations. The following sections will take a look at each scenario, including ideas to help you be prepared and cope with kindness when they occur.

Medical Note: Depending on the severity of your traumatic experiences, you might find it helpful to process these triggering situations with the help of a trauma-informed licensed medical professional.

Holiday Meals

Holidays and celebrations are a breeding ground for triggers because there are many variables surrounding food and eating. Concerns that you'll eat "too much," eat uncontrollably, be pressured to eat certain foods, or have your choices questioned commonly arise before a holiday meal. Visualize these potential situations beforehand, and remember to tune into your body and practice self-compassion.

Before the meal, take a minute to ground yourself. Take a few deep breaths. Remember that you are worthy and safe. Next, think of something that makes you feel grateful for this situation. It could be excitement about eating pecan pie or seeing your family for the first time in months. Finish by visualizing yourself peacefully enjoying what you want. Imagine having pleasant experiences with those you love.

Although grounding yourself isn't fail-proof, it can help you feel calmer going into the meal. Both gratitude and visualization have numerous advantages. For instance, visualization helps you mentally prepare and be more effective at problem solving. Practicing gratitude contributes to feeling more balanced with less depressive symptoms. Feeling more stable and less anxious helps you make decisions that support your body best.

When selecting what to eat, remind yourself that one meal is not going to make or break your health. Survey your options. What looks good to you right now? What foods make your taste buds jump with holiday spirit? Don't forget that you are free to eat anything, and it is completely up to you to decide what to feed your body.

These suggestions can help decrease the anxiety you feel in situations like holiday meals, but they will not make everything perfect. Unpleasant or uncomfortable situations may arise. Be sure to avoid setting unrealistic expectations when you practice visualization. For example, you might eat past fullness, or someone could rudely comment on your food choices. This is normal and to be expected. Everybody's got their stuff around food, and emotions are typically charged around the holidays.

If you feel triggered in the middle of the meal, practice grounding exercises like deep breathing or focusing on your food. Savor the food's aromas, appearance, textures, and flavors. Disengage with negative conversations around food guilt or body bashing. If you feel safe to do so, talk about how negative comments about your body make you feel. You could also ask your family or friends not to comment on your body.

Most important, continue caring for yourself. If self-care feels challenging at the moment, treat yourself like you'd treat a friend in the same situation. Feed your body in a way that feels good and meets your needs. Above all, remember that you deserve to eat and enjoy food. You are worthy of eating in peace, and you are allowed to eat what you want, eat more than others, stop when you want, and eat when others are not. You have permission to enjoy the holiday meal, regardless of your body or health.

Doctors' Offices

A visit to the doctor's office can be nerve-racking for many reasons. You might be worried that you'll be chastised for your weight or diagnosed with a life-altering medical condition. Several situations might, understandably, make you reluctant to get a checkup. Rethinking healthcare visits and preparing in advance can help.

You are the expert of your body. You know your body best. Healthcare practitioners are there to help you feel well and manage your health. The point of going to the doctor's office is to take care of yourself, not to please the doctor. Reframe your visit as a conversation between you and your healthcare practitioner. During this conversation, simply share your symptoms and ask questions to learn more about your health.

To avoid an unhelpful or distressing experience at the doctor's office, imagine yourself piloting a plane. Healthcare practitioners are flight attendants. They're making sure everyone stays safe and hydrated, while you are flying the plane and pushing buttons if anything goes wrong. (Clearly, my knowledge of piloting a plane is quite limited. Just go with it.) Flight attendants have an essential role yet cannot fly the plane. Your doctors have an important role in your health, but they are not in charge of you. Be the pilot of your own health.

Try removing some anxiety about an upcoming doctor's visit by preparing in advance. Know your symptoms and questions prior to your visit. Explore procedures or screenings you potentially need based on your age, preexisting health conditions, genetics, or symptoms. Advocate for your health or bring a supportive friend or family member to be your co-pilot.

Acknowledging our common humanity can be helpful. Healthcare practitioners are humans—very intelligent, caring ones—but still humans. So you might experience weight stigma in the doctor's office just like you will anywhere else. The prevalence of this stigma doesn't excuse this type of behavior from a healthcare practitioner, but it can help explain some of the negative feedback you receive.

If you have a larger body, you might have felt shamed because of your BMI, had your concerns dismissed because of your weight, or received criticism based solely on your size. This type of treatment can feel invalidating and dehumanizing, so it's normal to want to avoid healthcare visits. But getting your health checked is a form of self-nurturing behavior, and you deserve respectful care that is free of weight stigma no matter what your weight or health status is.

Acknowledge what could be triggering about the doctor's office before you go. For many people, being weighed causes anxiety. However, you can decline to be weighed unless medically necessary, for example, for determining medication dosages. Declining to be weighed might feel challenging, especially if you do not like confrontation. Yet it is your right to decline. Say something simple like, "I do not want to be weighed, thanks," and you can share any weight changes with your doctor if relevant. If you must be weighed, you can do a blind weighing and request the number be left off any documents shared with you.

If your healthcare provider recommends weight loss, ask them to show you peer-reviewed research that shows long-term safety and efficacy for weight loss (hint: it doesn't exist) or studies that directly link your condition to your weight. Also ask your provider what treatment ideas they would provide a straight-sized patient. Respectfully request evidence-based interventions.

In conclusion, the doctor's office is rife with triggers. Be prepared by knowing your reasons for the visit and remember that you are the expert of your body. You have a right to be treated with respect without discrimination based on your body size or health status. You deserve to take charge of your health with your healthcare practitioner by your side.

Social Situations

People want to feel and look their best in public, so both the social event and time leading up to one can be stressful. You might feel the need to impress others with how you look or worry that someone will think you've "let yourself go." You could receive triggering comments on how you look, what you're eating, your happiness, or your health.

To reduce the desire to change your body for an event, remember what is important to you. Continue to practice behaviors that feel good for your body. Keep meeting your needs instead of making choices that focus only on appearance or trying to reach some unrealistic standard.

While at an event, set boundaries around how you talk about food, bodies, and lifestyles. For example, ask friends not to discuss their diets, avoid conversations that bash bodies, or turn away anyone pressuring you to try their new workout plan. Diet talk is a common subject in social situations, so it is helpful to have boundaries and coping skills in place before you go.

Like all triggering situations, practicing self-compassion is essential, especially if you have a larger body or have gained weight. People with larger bodies are more susceptible to being stigmatized, questioned, ridiculed, and dehumanized. If you have a larger body, you will likely have less freedom, fewer resources, and fewer experiences to enjoy your body without judgment from others. Turning inward and practicing self-compassion can help you cope in any triggering situation.

Using a phrase from loving-kindness meditations could help you feel more grounded. Repeat any or all of these statements to yourself: "May I be safe. May I be peaceful. May I be kind to myself. May I accept myself as I am." These statements help you be kind to yourself, and remember the common humanity you share with those around you.

Work and School Stress

Stress can amplify almost any situation into a trigger. Whereas the aforementioned examples are related to triggers from outside sources, stress causes you to ignore self-care, lose insight into your internal cues, and resort to unhelpful coping techniques. For example, an upcoming project may have you staying up late at night, mindlessly eating snacks, and staring at a bright screen.

Remember what you have learned about consistently and adequately meeting your needs every single day. Though some days might be busier or more stressful than others, it's important that you continue to take care of yourself no matter what is happening in your life. Continue to practice your daily self-nurture routine (see here), even if it's an abbreviated version. Self-care will help you release tension without using unhelpful coping techniques.

No matter what, caring for yourself matters. Self-care will help protect you from repeatedly ignoring hunger cues. Restriction leads to overeating, overeating leads to guilt, and guilt leads you back to restriction—then the cycle starts all over again.

If you are feeling overwhelmed by anxiety at work, school, or home, it can be tempting to turn to controlling your body through food or exercise as a coping mechanism. However, recalling the pain these coping mechanisms have caused in the past can strengthen your resistance against the urge to control.

Remember that it's normal to ignore hunger cues because of stress, to resort to numbing your feelings with food, and to eat in excess when you've gone too long without food. These are not moral failings, and it's okay when they happen. Instead of letting this pattern continue, grant yourself grace, and take steps to make helpful choices next time.

Everyone's Triggers Are Different

Whatever triggers disrupt your practice of intuitive eating are valid, and they'll likely change along with you. Everyone and every day are different, so it's best to be prepared as much as possible for potential triggers. No matter what the trigger is, draw boundaries, map out how you'll deal with possible scenarios, have support, and treat yourself with self-compassion.

Start by creating personal boundaries to designate the behaviors you will or will not tolerate from others. Boundaries are vital for protection from potential problematic events. Recognize what upsets you and how you can draw boundaries in your life that protect you. Boundaries are not bad or inconsiderate; they simply keep you from allowing others or yourself to mistreat you.

Think about situations that could be problematic for you. Consider probable scenarios and run through what might happen and how you could effectively react. Decide on some possible coping techniques. Remember you are only in control of your own reactions, not the emotions you experience or how someone else feels, acts, or responds. This activity helps you be proactive about likely triggers instead of reacting in a way that is going to make you feel worse.

A support system can help you work through the scenarios, draw boundaries, and digest a triggering experience. Support can be found in friends, family, online communities, dietitians, therapists, certified intuitive eating counselors, or other weight-neutral health practitioners.

Furthermore, you are only in charge of you, so it's up to you to continue caring for yourself. Honor what is important to you and make choices that align with your values instead of being affected by what others think of you. Remember the truth about what happens to your body to prevent you from resorting to changing your body as a result of the negative stress of being triggered. Continue practicing self-compassion to keep from beating yourself up, feeling alone, getting carried away with your uncomfortable feelings, or overidentifying with your triggers.

Creating Boundaries

Drawing boundaries in your life is one of the best things you can do for yourself and those around you. Even though it can feel harsh or uncomfortable at first, establishing clear boundaries will help you be more emotionally healthy, which will strengthen your relationships and nurture others. It helps people understand how you want to be treated by giving them guidelines for the behaviors you believe are acceptable and unacceptable.

Boundaries need to be clear and firm, but if setting them intimidates you, remember that they are not permanent. Think of boundaries like a wooden fence in your yard. In a few years, your fence might need to be updated. Maybe you want to move the fence, paint it, or replace some broken places. Boundaries are not a concrete wall. They are not all or nothing, always or never.

To create boundaries, assess the areas of your life that feel uncomfortable or problematic. Base boundaries around your time, energy, values, emotions, and physical body. Decide what you need to keep yourself safe and at peace. Be direct and respectful. Make your request, and be sure to follow through. Set consequences for potential boundary breakers. You can give a reason why this boundary is important to you, but you do not need to overexplain yourself.

For example, you might have a boundary that you don't talk negatively about food. A potential option to enforce this boundary is directly stating your desire by saying, "I'd love to enjoy my meal in peace. Is it possible for us not to discuss guilt around food?" Other options are to change the subject, excuse yourself from the table, or mentally remove yourself from the conversation by practicing mindfulness or breathing exercises. Try the grounding 54321 method: Notice five things you can see, four you can touch, three you can hear, two you can smell, and one you can taste.

Know that if someone has been excessively relying on you, taking advantage of you, or treating you poorly, a boundary will initially feel challenging for them. They might feel like you are being self-centered or letting them down. Remember that their feelings are not your responsibility. Your own well-being is the priority, and you are not being selfish by asking them to respect your wishes.

Intuitive Eating Is a Lifestyle

The work doesn't stop after learning all the principles, but your new skills and knowledge will help you continue the path of living a life using your own wisdom and experience. Though many diets claim to be a lifestyle, intuitive eating actually is one. The 10 principles of intuitive eating are simply guides, so there is no right or wrong way to practice intuitive eating. Just like we are all unique people, we all interpret intuitive eating a little differently.

You will find that the principles apply to other areas of your life, and they also build upon each other. Even when you encounter body changes, triggering situations, or boundary violations, you have the skills you need to keep living in line with your values.

The flexible nature of intuitive eating allows you to grow and change while still emphasizing what matters to you in each season of life. Some principles of intuitive eating might be more applicable to you now than they will be in 10 years, but you will always have this internal wisdom to guide you in living a life that focuses on holistic health and well-being.

Conclusion

All facets of health are important: physical, mental, emotional, and spiritual. Our life is richest when we allow space for every aspect of our health to be nurtured in a way that feels best for our body. There will always be outside influences that attempt to guide you on how to live, but you are the only one who knows how to live a life true to you. Perhaps it's scary to think that your body could gain weight because diet culture makes it difficult for people with larger bodies to feel accepted. But practicing self-compassion can help you cope with weight changes. And remember that no matter the situation, be sure to have clear boundaries, prepare for potential triggering scenarios, make choices that align with your values, and take care of yourself.